This 2018 map secthe Jicarilla Indian reservation's 'ts of Carson NF. The Continental Divide is snown in the right-hand third of this map segment. Highway 550, out of Cuba, intersects with north-bound 537 just inside the reservation and 537 intersects and ends at Highway 64 in the north part of the reservation. Note that Highway 537 makes two major curves. The sawmill site was about four or five miles northwest of the second curve (northbound) apex. It is important to know that Highways 550, 537 and 64 represent the majority of paved roads in the reservation.

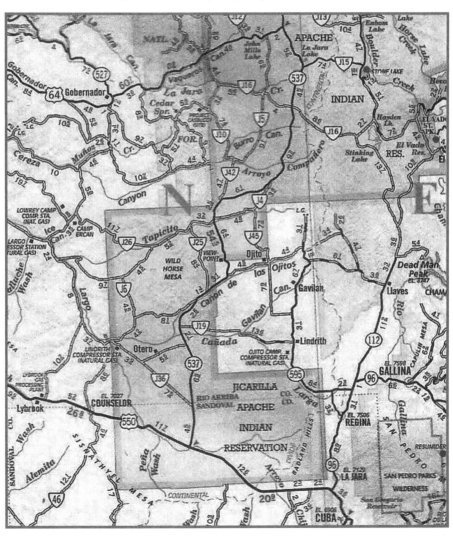

A 1950 map of NW New Mexico. Bernalillo (just north and a little east of Albuquerque is the beginning of route 44 (Highway 550 today) going northwest to Aztec. Before Aztec, find route 17 (now Highway 64) that eastbound goes into Dulce inside the Jicarilla Apache Reservation. Where Highway 17 crosses into the Apache Reservation, follow the reservation boundary line southward to a penciled in dot. The area you are in at that point is today designated as a section of Carson National Forest and the dot represents the approximate location of the sawmill site of this story.

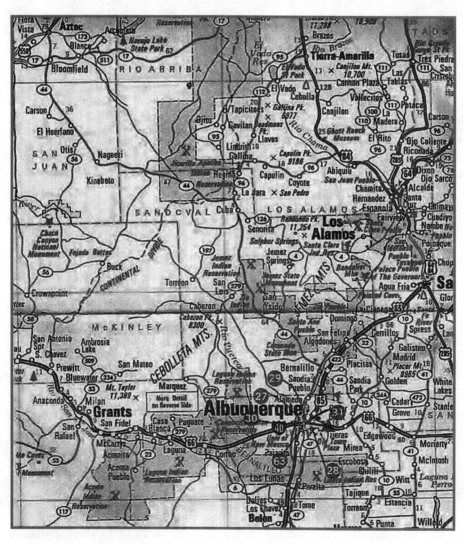

The SAWMILL

A NEW
BEGINNING

SAWMILL AREA IN 2018

Up the hill from canyon rim area is the cabin and corral area

In 1950 four small, rustic shacks were situated along the tree line. The trees you see here are much newer growth, older trees having been harvested, but the view is not much different, if any. The corral was situated about where the clear area is on the upper right. Sawmill machinery, dock area, and scrap lumber storage areas were to the right of the photographer – as is the canyon rim. The view in this image is toward the northwest. The canyon rim was to the photographer's right, perhaps forty or fifty yards away, with the mill equipment installed right on the edge of the rim so the sawdust could be directed into the canyon. Our "living accommodations" were situated in a quarter-circle fashion with the "kitchen" cabin on the left looking south and the fourth cabin on the right looking east across the canyon.

To the east in the canyon floor is the fenced boundary separating Carson NF from the Jicarilla Apache reservation as it is today and was in 1950. Carson NF was established in 1908 but it seems road maps in the 1950s do not always detail National Forest boundaries. Also, in 1950, no fence separated Carson NF from the reservation grounds. I think we were unaware we were living in a National Forest.

------------------------------- ❋ -------------------------------

The SAWMILL

A NEW BEGINNING

CLAUDE ROMACK

dustjacket

©2019 Published by Dust Jacket Press
The Sawmill: A New Beginning / Claude Romack

ISBN: 978-1-947671-68-3

Dust Jacket Press
P.O. Box 721243
Oklahoma City, OK 73172
www.dustjacket.com

Cover and interior design by D. E. West, ZAQ Designs & Dust Jacket Creative Services

Printed in the United States of America

www.dustjacket.com

DEDICATION

To the memory of our son Michael Douglas Romack (1959 – 1991) whom Bonnie and I loved deeply and admired tremendously through his too-short life. He honored me and made me proud when he followed in my footsteps into the pharmaceutical world. He made Bonnie and me proud grandparents to two children, Courtney and Brian. Michael's love of sports gave him the ability to focus clearly and practice hard in his quest for honor and perfection throughout his life. His abilities to focus and to "take charge" enabled him to set and achieve worthwhile goals for himself and his family. Bonnie and I will never know for sure, in our time on earth, the reason or reasons that caused him to take his own life. What we do know, however, is that he is at peace in his rest with Christ Jesus. May God bless his soul.

To the memory of my brother Michael Ray Romack (1940 – 1997) whom I loved and respected; especially his intelligence, wit, and humor. Together we shared hard and difficult childhoods that could have resulted in unfortunate and even more difficult times had a higher power not intervened. Mike, in his adulthood, suffered the loss of two children. I believe, however, that he had several good years in terms of family living and productive work. But he died with lung cancer at age fifty-seven. In one of our more serious moments years ago during a family gathering while discussing "the good ole' days," he looked at me and said in a very firm and calm voice, "We went through a lot of 'real bad stuff' together, didn't we? But we made it."

———————— ❋ ————————

TABLE OF CONTENTS

PART I: GROWING UP

Early childhood years living in Colorado and New Mexico. Stories consistent with activities, mistakes, blunders and general behavior (good and bad) of two boys from ages 3 and 4 up to 9 1/2 and near 11 years. The house fire changes everything.

PART II: WORK IN THE WILDERNESS

The two brothers and their two sisters, ages 5 and newborn, find themselves living in the north-central mountains of New Mexico in rustic shacks with wood-burning stoves and coal oil lanterns. Poor daily living conditions added considerable discomfort and challenges. The boys harvested the trees, removed the limbs, and cut the trunks into sections for transport to the mill, not with power saws, but with crosscut saws and double-bit axes. Duration at the sawmill was fifteen or sixteen months. Some would say it must have seemed like a lifetime.

PART III: WORK, SCHOOL AND THE TRIAL

We four siblings had no recall of the journey from the mountains of New Mexico to Pawnee Oklahoma in early Fall of 1951. A primary concern Mike and I shared was the possibility of being a year older than our classmates since we missed a full year (plus some). The need for each of us to find ways to earn spending money came as no real surprise and we did well. We had some good times during school, but more trouble was yet ahead.

PART IV: WORK AND FAMILY

A quickly arranged wedding after attending court trial proceedings sounds like possible makings of a good soap-opera! Instead, it turned out to be a life-long adventure with bumps in the road, some smooth places and spectacular high points. But, now, in our early eighties we get to go more, read more, do more photography and tend to our aches and pains. Oh, and get some retirement money each month too! How nice!

INTRODUCTION

ABOUT THIS STORY

The Sawmill is presented, primarily, in first-person narrative (style, fashion, format) choose the word you like! The actual "story" part begins in Chapter 1. Here I present some information for you to have in mind as you read through the "nuts and bolts" of this close and personal story. You will read the story of the very young years of my siblings and me and, very likely, begin to sense the tone of the rest of the story. These first seven chapters reveal some of the activities and circumstances that shaped the early years of our lives.

Part 1 concludes with the story of the house fire which, in retrospect, seems to have been a forecast of the radical and totally unexpected series of events that followed. And looking back after many, many years, it seems to have become obvious that the house fire seriously impacted our lives. But that impact didn't really become obvious to any of us until we were in our twenties and thirties. In later years as I looked back on some of those events, my brother and I became more and more convinced that the house fire was intentionally set. So, as you venture into this book, take a few moments from time to time to study the map pages and think about living in an area with few paved roads, lots of hills, canyons, trees and wildlife – even today. And picture yourself in those areas with no running well water, no electricity, no heat source except for wood-fueled fires and living in backwoods shacks.

Almost every time I began to write more of this story, images of the mill site appeared in my mind. Memories of the hard work and unacceptable behavior of a mean and cruel male stepparent often occupied my thoughts. However, rather than dread my writing, the memories and images spurred me on and enhanced my focus. For topographical references go to a web site, like Google Earth, or EARTH maps satellite, which will take you to your present location when you log in. Then focus in order to identify highways and towns/cities. Scroll in the appropriate direction to reach northwest New Mexico. Find Cuba, NM on Highway 550 about 140 miles northwest of Albuquerque. Then find Highway 537 going north off 550. Reference the provided map in this book and locate the highways and other indicators and you'll get a sense of the remoteness even today in 2019. You'll want to look for the two large curves in the highway to the right (northbound) and center on the second curve. At that point you are within 4 or 5 miles of the sawmill site. You'll see metal buildings, fence rows, trucks and pick-ups, etc. at that second curve to the right. Road 314 (a dirt road) will take you into that farthest northwest section of Carson National Forest, and you will be inside the NF boundaries when you cross over a cattle-guard opening in the fence line.

Road 314 then meanders westerly for about a mile, then turns northeast into Glenwood Canyon (we saw a sign at that turn identifying the canyon) where you can go as far as the last (at that time – 2018) gas well location. Park in a safe place that doesn't interfere with the gas trucks. Then, on foot, go under or around the locked gate and hike about another 1.5 to 2 miles to Iron Spring canyon area. You'll not have any signs identifying the canyon, but at that point you'll see large areas of bare rock surfaces that will allow you to look down into the canyon. You might also be able to access the Iron Spring area – in the canyon bottom. Also, the National Forest fence line runs north/south in about the center of the canyon floor. A high level of grass and tree growth in the canyon probably identifies the area of the spring (which is now <u>fresh</u> water). The road from the gate where you park your vehicle tends to go straight north. So, when you reach that last well-site (you'll run out of road at that point), make your bearing east-northeast. If you continue straight north, all you'll be doing is hiking parallel with the canyon. PLEASE DO NOT attempt this trip without proper preparation. Altitude is about 8000 feet, and summer weather can be in the nineties to low 100s. Spring and fall cooler – a lot! I've been told by a local guide that black bears are common in the area now. Also, even if you have a "good sense of direction" – take a compass and use it! For a little more perspective, Road 314 enters the National Forest grounds at the extreme southeast corner through a cattle guard gate. If you were to follow the fence line straight north, you would eventually (about two or three miles) find yourself near the Iron Spring area and could see the rock cliff areas on the west side of the canyon. Also, at that point it is/was possible to get to the top of the canyon wall via an accessible-by-foot area a bit north of the spring area. We used to take our horses up and down that "ramp" area. You'll find more information about this area in Chapters 8 and 9.

Part II will describe, in limited detail, various aspects of our living, working, and playing during our fifteen or sixteen months in the mountains of north-central New Mexico in 1950 and 1951. Some of the events I'll present to you will probably look and "sound" like very extreme circumstances. However, historically speaking, many of these happenings presented herein are not new to humanity in general and American history specifically. Millions of young folks have lived and worked under conditions that, today, may look and sound like something criminally or inhumanely applied and put in place but that were perceived then to be acceptable. My siblings and I were, indeed, subjected to punishment methods that, today, are simply not acceptable or condoned. But when broken skin, black eyes, damaged extremities, and treatment like being chained to a tree or subjected to extreme temperatures (cold or hot) for long periods without relief, are put in place, they demand attention. While those measures were used in those years, it seems common use of them was not particularly widespread. One of my concerns in later years during the time when my relationship with Bonnie became much more serious, I began to wonder about whether I should even attempt to "start a family." Aspects of this are discussed a bit more in Part IV. Today, though, we believe our marriage, which has had it "ups and downs," has strengthened significantly in numerous and varied ways. Finally, I must confirm that God has blessed me with an incredibly strong woman for my life mate. Thus, I give God my undying thanks. Part III focuses on our activities, issues and problems of living "back among the civilized" again. We had issues of school related activities, learning how to be civilized again, and work issues. Some things seemed to repeat in some ways many of the things we dealt with at the sawmill. Others were simply new things impacting our lives, some good, some not so good.

Part IV excludes a lot of detail but does connect, at least in some ways, issues of the past with current issues. It also makes clear that life does go on and things can and do change, often for the better. Absolutely, events at the sawmill impacted the lives of my siblings, my mother, and me in many ways; some of which we do not necessarily care to discuss. It does seem reasonable to conclude that we all experienced a certain kind and amount of "growing up" that we may never have experienced under normal (whatever normal means) circumstances. I am certain, however, that we would have preferred to achieve many of those experiences in some other fashion!

For some, this story might put into perspective the importance of various things and happenings people encounter and experience from time to time. Most Americans today live lives of relative comfort and productivity; relatively few can imagine anything otherwise. However, life on The Sawmill in the mountains of northern New Mexico in 1950, as seen through the eyes of an eleven-year-old boy, provided few, if any, creature comforts. We had very few regular meals, no security, no entertainment, and no Sunday afternoon strolls; we kids did have plenty of work and, fortunately, or perhaps unfortunately, some early lessons about life, living, struggling, and surviving. In the years immediately following the end of WWII, when the country was again experiencing optimism and some amount of good fortune and was still reveling in our victories over Germany and Japan, but becoming embroiled in Korea, many areas of our country were still uninhabited, unknown and remote. To the common American citizen, the place at the sawmill was certainly largely unknown and very certainly remote, although considerably less so today. Being frightened, for us kids, was part of our lives while we were in the wilderness of New Mexico's northern mountains, a little west of the continental divide. My brother, about a year and a half younger than I and our two sisters both younger than we two boys, found ourselves living in a world different from that to which we had become accustomed. Many memories and happenings of that place and time, in the main for me, seem relatively clear. However, many other memories, I am certain, have been blocked. My brother, whom we lost in 1997, and I, could, in later years recall many events and circumstances of the time. The older of my two sisters also has clear recollection of many events of the time while the younger sister, being a newborn, obviously has no recollection of our time in the mountains of northwestern New Mexico.Some wise person has, at some time or other, said something like, "it is best for some things to be forgotten." Often, however, it is that some things are simply not forgettable and even should be remembered. And that's primarily the "why" of this story. For it is the shared memories of certain significant events and circumstances of four siblings. We did not forget. Not on your life! Unfortunately, parental abuse is not uncommon. It is probably so in every part of the world and not just "back then." Will it ever stop here on earth? Most likely not. But we can pray for and support victims of parental abuse. It is the hope of my sisters, my wife and me, that this story will illustrate that God does indeed look after us and help and guide us. So, read the story and judge for yourself. Let your conscience and your own life experiences be your reference points. And say a prayer of thanks for our relatively good outcomes, but more importantly, a prayer of hope and support for millions of young people around the world who suffer every day, oftentimes at the hands of their own family members and "friends," and in ways many of us cannot imagine.

Worship of the Lord had never been part of my life until my middle teen years. Becoming a Christian happened in my sophomore year in school because most of my friends were "church goers," and I wanted to be part of that fellowship. It's wonderful how that happens sometimes, isn't it? And I believe it is part of God's plan that this story has found its way into a book. My use of scripture at or near the beginning of several chapters and sections is intended primarily to help keep the story focused on the idea that a person's belief system can go a long way toward helping with recovery from negative and catastrophic impacts, but in a positive way. Humor is my other "crutch." A little chuckle, or a smile, or out-loud laughter, I believe to be healthy. I also believe some lightheartedness in the right places helps us understand and cope better. I hope you experience that as you read through *The Sawmill*. So, get your light right, your comfort level to your satisfaction, and enjoy this read. And a big THANKS! to my proofreaders, Becky, Fran, Mary, Kent, Bill, Shirleen, and Donna. Some were pretty tough. Some were kinda bossy. They were all quite correct!

THANKS TO MR. & MRS. LARRY NELSON

A note sent to "Postmaster, Ojito, NM" in mid 2017 resulted in my contact with the Nelson family in Lindrith, NM. Their daughter, the postmistress in Lindrith, received my note sent to Ojito which no longer has a post office. She gave my note to Mr. Nelson with the agreement that he would follow-up, which he did. He first sent a letter explaining the above, and this then precipitated dialog via letters and phone calls that enabled Bonnie and me to eventually find the actual location (area) of the sawmill above Iron Spring canyon just inside the far-western section of Carson National Forest.

Entrance to Nelson Ranch, North of Lindrith, NM

Part I
Growing Up

CHAPTER 1

Hot? Cold? Or Just Lukewarm?

I know your works, that you are neither cold nor hot.
I could wish you were cold or hot. So then, because you are lukewarm,
and neither cold nor hot, I will vomit you out of My mouth.
Revelation 3:15-16 (NKJV)

When considering the words "hot" and "cold" in this scriptural context, one quickly becomes informed in Revelation 3:15-16 that we are talking about being hot or cold for Jesus Christ. John tells us it is better to be hot or cold in order that we are not just lukewarm. So, perhaps it is that if you have experienced the good "hot" of a really good chili pepper or a steaming bowl of soup, then you might have a good idea of what it is, or could be, to experience the "hot" of a relationship with Jesus Christ.

I believe that if my immediate family in my early childhood had been living and continued to live as followers of Jesus Christ, in other words, "Hot;" that much of the negative aspects of what follows in this story would never have happened and consequently not ever written about. I am not prepared to say that my family was totally cold toward Jesus Christ,

1

but I can say that living for Christ was very certainly not on our priority list until much later.

PLACE OF BIRTH AND A NICKNAME

May 28, 1939 was the day of my introduction to life. I was told, by people who knew, like my mother and some aunts and uncles, that the day of my entry into the world was also the day I was given my nickname "Pinky." And the nickname was established within seconds of my official birth time! That moniker did not become a part of my birth documents, but it did become a part of my entire life. And I've certainly had a few occasions when I found it necessary to defend the nickname. Many of my extended family today find it a bit uncomfortable when asked about my "real" name when they must pause to think about the answer. The name "Claude" seems to not always come immediately to mind. Oh well, such is life sometimes! Approximately eighteen months later came the birth of my brother Michael, also in Colorado Springs. His nickname "Mike" was easy and uncomplicated. He never had to "explain" or defend it. He neither received nor caused a bloody nose over it. Added to my siblings list are two females who, at first were once little girls, now they are both grandmothers with children and grandchildren who all seem to be involved in many different vocations and avocations. They all live honorably and pay taxes. Everybody seems to have something worthwhile to do to earn their livings. I'm proud of them all! Well, so here we were, in Colorado Springs, (actually we were in a little place called Palmer Lake, about twenty miles north of Colorado Springs) Colorado, enjoying winter weather and mild summer temperatures and thin air. Although I have no actual memory of any of that, so I guess my statement is simply an assumption. Following a few clues and answers to questions, I discovered that my family was in Colorado for two primary reasons: 1) extended family lived in the area, and 2) men of the families all had jobs in and around Colorado Springs. The jobs held by my father and two uncles on Mom's side were auto mechanics working in local shops and/or for many of the racecar drivers who flooded into Colorado Springs to compete in the very popular annual Pike's Peak racing event. This racing event is known as the "Race to the Clouds." The road up to the top is 12.5 miles with 156 turns. This annual event started in 1916. These connections eventually, late in 1942, caused the migration of my father and both uncles and their families to Albuquerque, New Mexico. I do not know factually the reason for this relocation, but rationale suggests that it was most likely due to Albuquerque being more central to many of the racing venues of the region, and more of the racing teams were locating in Albuquerque. I was probably about three and a half by that time. And, so it was that sister Mary Sue was born in April 1943 in Albuquerque.

MY FATHER DEPARTED

As far as I can determine, my father deserted us likely a few months before the birth of Mary Sue. If my brother, Mike, were still alive, he could help me understand the disposition of our father since Mike became somewhat involved with him in later years. I dislike even thinking about this, but I have believed for a long time that the desertion was to avoid military duty, considering the U.S. had become actively involved in WWII by then. If that is so, then shame on him! My sense is that all of us kids, from that point, lived rather uncertain lives for quite some time, moving from place to place, keeping ahead of the rent collectors – because mom had three children and no regular job. The time when my father acted on the decision that he no longer wanted to be a part of our family, as well as, perhaps, the United States Military, I am not totally clear about. But it was most likely very late in 1942 or early 1943. For certain, it was before Mary Sue's birth in April and my fourth birthday in May of 1943. The problematic and obvious result of this separation was that mom, with three kids and very little, if any, income, moved around often; primarily, I think, to avoid rent payments. She had no job, no husband, and three kids. Of course, Mom's brother and one of her sisters and their families, also living in Albuquerque, meant Mom had at least a little bit of help and support. She still needed to and did, eventually, find a job. These issues contributed to the need, as mentioned earlier, for us to move frequently. I have recollections of living with our maternal grandparents, with an aunt and uncle, and by ourselves in several places in Albuquerque. I recall a small adobe structure and a couple of small apartment units, one place with dirt floors, rats and lizards, as well as a place with a garden of red, yellow and orange chili peppers and a lot of pear cactus in various clusters in the dirt yard. Look for more on the peppers and cactus a little later in this chapter.

Here is a snippet about a high-desert danger. Following the departure of our father, Mom, having a rough time just making ends meet, lived off and on with our grandparents in a somewhat even more remote area northwest of Albuquerque. It seems that one very late spring or early summer afternoon in 1943, when the day had warmed up and the sun was in the west over the volcanos, brother Mike spotted what he thought was a turtle. It was sunning itself while lying on the inside of an upturned and empty wooden orange crate and fully exposed to the afternoon sun. This is what I remember about what happened: I noticed Mike's interest in what he was calling a "turtle." When I saw that what he was heading for was not a turtle, but a coiled-up rattlesnake, I ran and grabbed Mike and pulled him into the house and went hollering for Grandma and Grandpa. Grandma found a hoe, went to the orange crate, pulled the snake out and killed it. It seemed almost like something she did every day. No excitement. No hollering. No panic. No scolding. She just did the job. Amazing! All that activity is possibly what allowed Mike to achieve his third birthday in November 1943! It was in one of those places during our "moving around" when we were with an uncle and his family, that I saw, and was deeply impressed, by the cover photograph of either a "Life" or "Saturday Evening Post" magazine. The cover photo featured a U.S. soldier, standing, I believe, among several downed soldiers. His left hand was over his eyes, head bowed, his rifle gripped in his right hand hanging by his side. The horrors of war! I have since sometimes wondered if that magazine news article was a product of Albuquerque-based news correspondent Ernie Pyle. Remembering my father is quite difficult since he left Mom and we three children sometime before my fourth birthday. Mike would have been a little over two and Mary Sue unborn. The fact is, I never came to know him in any way. One of our old photo albums has a small picture of my father when I was about two. If we were together today, we would look almost identical, I believe. Those photographs, when compared with photos of myself at approximately the same age, reveal remarkably similar body and facial features. I have vague recollections of his laughter, which I believe I have essentially mimicked. Overheard discussions between two of my uncles in the past have revealed that my father was a good mechanic and that they all worked in auto mechanic shops as well as in the racecar maintenance business. My brother, Mike, was able to develop a relationship of sorts with him sometime in the 1960s and early 70s. At that time, Mike lived in south Colorado Springs and worked as a machine shop mechanic. I remember my own negative actions and behavior upon hearing of him or his name in discussions with Mike.

In my high school years, I came to resent him very much because his vacancy in our family was filled by X whom you'll meet later. And I have, from time to time, reminisced about what life could have been like if he had stayed around. Obsession with any of this I believe has not happened. But sometimes in those years, remorse seems to have set in causing me to think about how different life could have been. That may have been on my mind when in 1967, following my return from Vietnam, he showed up at the front door of our house on Lampson Avenue in Garden Grove, California. All of us Romack men seem to have fairly strong familial facial features, so I recognized him as I opened the front door when he knocked. I just simply and softly closed the door and set the lock. He didn't knock again. And, I never saw him again. He likely found my name and address in the Garden Grove phone book.

After we moved to Delaware a few years later, I heard from Mom that he had died. I remember feeling a deep sadness which, I believe, was probably more about me than about my father. I think that may have been the first time I fully realized and thought about the fact that Mary Sue, Mike, and I all grew up and achieved adulthood without a full-time real "father" figure. That fact comes into much sharper focus beginning in Chapter 5. Sister Donna June, whom you have yet to meet, fared better, having been fortunate enough to experience a great relationship with Mom's last marriage to "Pappy" (as brother Mike and I most often addressed him). His name was Dick Hinds. We all loved and respected him. He was a top-notch mechanic and a decorated World War II veteran. He was also an accomplished fisherman who built his own really terrific pontoon boat, a boat built just for the Tulsa area lakes!

THE DOG BITE AND FIRST SCAR

At the ripe old age of perhaps three and a half, not long after we arrived in Albuquerque from Colorado Springs in late 1942, and before sister Mary Sue's birth and our father's desertion in 1943, I received the first injury that left a scar which is still quite visible as I achieve the "riper" old age of eighty. My presumption is that in my quest to give a pet dog a hug, I hugged too tightly. He bit me! On my nose! The original scar was from the bridge of my nose down to the outside of the right nostril and into my cheek. Just about a half inch of scar remains today. Skin cancer surgeries have since removed all the old scar tissue from the dog bite, except for that portion by the nostril on my cheek. But now I have scar tissue from the skin cancer repairs!

My father, who was still with us, immediately collared the dog, took him out into the higher desert area northwest of Albuquerque, somewhere near those dormant volcanos that are so clearly visible from most parts of town even today, and shot it. I have no memory of what the dog looked like, its breed, whether it was male or female, or its name. I just remember the dog bite and the dog being taken away. The remaining scar from the bite, although not huge, is still quite visible and seems to stand out – especially if my face is flushed from exertion or too much sunshine, or maybe embarrassment. And being a "red-head" (well, I used to be!) my "flushing," or, if you prefer, "blushing," is always quick and very obvious. My brother Mike and newborn baby sister Mary Sue, and I, after our father departed, lived with our mother in a little house along Route 66 out on what was then the western edge of Albuquerque near the bottom of "nine mile" hill close to the intersection of what is now Unser Boulevard. We had neighbors across the highway, but to the west and north was only sage brush, sand and those, I believe, five, dormant volcanos, that are dominant Albuquerque landmarks.

AIRCRAFT CRASH WITNESSED

I cannot specify time or date of the Military aircraft crash, but it would most likely, but not necessarily, have been in mid to late 1944 or early 1945. Kirtland AFB was, I believe, established in the early 1930s (or near that time frame); and we watched aircraft fly over often, obviously because of the very high activity of bombers and other military aircraft during WWII.

7

It was, I suppose, with a great amount of wonder that I watched one of those airplanes, a large multiple engine aircraft, fall out of the sky. I'm just guessing here, but because the aircraft was not very high off the ground, most likely, it had just taken off from Kirtland AFB. It was in a cluster of five or six aircraft and headed west paralleling Highway 66. I saw what I believe was smoke from one of the engines. Then the sound of the airplane changed, and it sort of wobbled and went into a straight down spinning fall. The crash site seems to have been on the north side of Highway 66, maybe almost on top of "nine mile" hill. I watched as it hit the earth and then saw a plume of black smoke rise slowly into the blue sky. Not long after, several other aircraft were circling the area and a group of military vehicles sped past our little house. I was only a little over five years of age at the time, but the image of the plane falling is still clear in my memory.

A site online that has catalogued military aircraft accidents and crashes revealed only one crash that might be consistent with time and place of the one I saw. It was a crash of a B29 in 1945 that had engine failure as it took off from Kirtland AFB. This 1945 documented crash data seems compatible with my memory of the event except the timing seems different. The documentation does not reveal the specific place/site of the crash. Perhaps a reader of this information could clarify the details of this event. Also, of interest would be information that might confirm date and place of a crash in the same general area, but at least several months or a year earlier. My memory of the event I witnessed seems more consistent with 1944 because I clearly recall watching from just off Highway 66. By 1945 we were living in some other part of Albuquerque. Again, if memory serves correctly!

CACTUS AND CHILI PEPPERS

Here's the fulfillment of my promise a few pages back to address the "Chili Peppers and Cactus" event. My brother and I both had moderately serious problems in the place with the peppers and cactus in the yard. I believe this might have been the beginning of the maturing process of the brains of both of us. But since I am quite, well almost, certain that both happenings I'm going to tell you about were his ideas, my laying the blame on him for the results of those misadventures among the cactus and hot peppers is (possibly) clearly justified! First has to do with the time Mike encouraged me to "help" him ride on the back of a quite large dog, a dog with short, slick hair. This was a very friendly dog that belonged to the man that owned the little two-room rental unit. That adventure ended when the dog dumped both of us into a patch of "pear" cactus.

It isn't so much the big cactus spines that hurt (although they did); it is more the problem of finding all those very tiny stickers (glochids) that appear in clusters, sometimes around the bases of the much larger spines on cactus plants. The only way Mom could find many of them was by feel – which only added to the agony! The search for the stickers and then removing them was as bad as getting the stickers in the first place! And, dear reader, please know (if you don't already) that preparations like topical hydrocortisone or any of the topical anesthetics were not commonly available (if at all) in those years. Not even topical antibiotics would have been available. Possibly penicillin, but probably not even that as a topical preparation. All we had was mineral oil or petroleum jelly and maybe Vicks or perhaps some kind of hand lotion and water. But whatever the "cure" might have been, it is with a high degree of certainty that I tell you we were removing sticker spines and burrs for weeks afterward. Often, when we thought we had gotten them all, more would surface, much to our amazement and disappointment, albeit ultimate relief.

The other misadventure happened as the chili peppers began to "come into season," the ripening causing their colors to become bright and intense. Those were what some call banana peppers, or a variation thereof. The bright yellow, red, and orange peppers, being quite attention getting with the dark green plant leaves as their background, certainly got our attention! Little kids, it seems, are unable to refrain from touching and handling those irresistible plants. I think we didn't just "touch" them, I believe we may have "caressed" them and pressed them to our faces. Their kind of oily or slick texture was quite inviting and, early on, made the skin of our hands and faces feel smooth and pliable. Soon, however, our faces and hands began to experience some irritation which then compels one to start scratching the exposed skin. And then, other parts of the body become involved when you scratch elsewhere. And it takes only one scratch to start it!

I do not recall for certain whether either of us needed to "take a leak" at some point, but it wouldn't surprise me if one of us did. When one has attained that point of this relationship with the peppers, one starts making a kind of fist in order to massage the eyes that have begun to itch. And that then, is when you are in way over your head. It's too late to avoid the pain and discomfort. You begin to panic in your search for relief. One is compelled to try anything, whether it sounds reasonable or not. But, whatever you do, little boy, do not go take a leak for you are dealing with a "danger factor" here!

Water didn't seem to help very much, but that was all we had at our disposal until somebody said "try milk". It is probable that some kind soul gave Mom some milk because, I am sure, we didn't have money to buy enough to satisfy our rather immediate needs. Whether it was the milk or time or something else, the burning eventually subsided, and we forgot all about it, until right now as I try to recapture bits of it! However, (and let me be clear about this) one must experience it to really understand the depth and complexity of the agony of chili pepper burns – especially those in your nose, mouth and eyes – and the cactus spine pricks. I have always believed that the forgetting of the experience is part of a natural defense mechanism God gives us to help us avoid serious mental problems. I say that as I reach to scratch another itch hoping the itch doesn't spread and believing it started when I started writing this scene. My, oh my! How powerful is the power of suggestion!?

Colorado Springs

…But you who fear my name, the Sun of righteousness shall arise with healing in His wings; And you shall go out and grow fat like stall-fed calves.

The people who fear God's name will see a new day. The Sun of Righteousness depicts the restoration of God's blessings and joy.

Malachi 4:2 (NKJV)

My sense is that our father having deserted us cast a shadow over Mom and her little family of three kids, sister Mary Sue still a baby. I believe her parents, my grandparents Plunkett, were still living in Palmer Lake, thereby being a magnet for Mom's decision to move back. Maybe this move looked like a good opportunity to enjoy the blessings of a new day. Maybe she just needed to be away from the Albuquerque area, thus away from reminders of her past situation.

PALMER LAKE

To tell you a specific time and date of our moving back to Colorado from Albuquerque is not possible because I simply do not know. I can say that it was likely sometime either side of my fifth birthday. I know I attended my first year of school in Palmer Lake which was the hometown of my grandparents Romack, whom I never really got to know. My maternal grandparents, E. J. and Bessie Plunkett also lived close by in Palmer Lake. Grandpa Plunkett was part of a railroad work force, a job that took him to Palmer Lake from Albuquerque. Palmer Lake was then, and is today, a suburb of Colorado Springs as noted earlier. I'm told, however, that since the establishment of the U.S. Air Force Academy is nearby, a lot of U.S. Air Force "brass" live in Palmer Lake along with many corporate executive types. How things change!

I do not recall anything of significance about my paternal grandparents during my very young years except that they lived in Palmer Lake and they raised foxes. Oddly, I do not remember ever receiving a fox garment, like a stole or a vest or scarf or hat of any description. Oh well! One can hope. Vague images of my riding in a horse-drawn feed wagon surface occasionally. This was the method for visiting each fox cage to feed and water them. The strongest of those memories is the strange, but not unpleasant, odors of the feed and foxes and horse droppings.

It was in the later part of this time that I entered my first year of school. So here we were now in Palmer Lake, Colorado, presumably because Mom had run out of resources in Albuquerque, needed help, and relocated close to her parents and other family who had also migrated north to follow the work availability. Therefore, Mike, baby sister Mary Sue, and I became acquainted with some of the Romack side of the family as well as Mom's parents and siblings. Here's a little "snippet" about Grandma Romack: Years later, after I joined the Navy, we began receiving "newsletters" from Grandma Romack that commented on her travel adventures in those last several years of her life. She started every one of them with, "Well, I'm still here," and would then continue with her always pleasant and informative message. I believe she celebrated her one-hundredth birthday a couple of years before her death. So, my brother, my sisters, and I were blessed, in those later years, to have had some form of communication from our paternal grandparents, following several decades of no contact with them.

Following are a few accounts of some of our adventures, conditions, and happenings in Palmer Lake, Colorado during that period in mid-to-late 1945 and most of 1946 while I was in my first year of formal education.

CHEWING TOBACCO

Palmer Lake was, for a short time as mentioned earlier, also the home of my maternal grandparents who, by the way, both used chewing tobacco. But this story actually took place several years later in my High School years. And it involves my life mate, Bonnie, when she and I were dating and going to high school in Pawnee, Oklahoma, in 1951 through 1957. Bonnie had been invited by Grandma Plunkett to come have lunch with her. After the meal, they moved to the living room to continue the visit. Bonnie then became confused about Grandma's frequent trips from her chair in the living room to the kitchen. So, Bonnie's catlike curiosity and her easy ability to ask questions and make comments other people wouldn't, caused her to ask about it. Grandma simply said, "Well, I chew so I must go and spit from time to time. It's not healthy to swallow that stuff, you know." Bonnie said, in reflection, that she almost fell out of her chair, and she'd "never ever" seen nor heard of anything like that! A woman. Chewing tobacco! And spitting! I believe I am correct in recollecting information that my grandparents Plunkett were both born and raised in Arkansas. For whatever that information might be worth!

GRANDPA'S STICK-SHIFT SKULL

In those mid 1940s when we lived in Palmer Lake Mike and I often rode in Grandpa's 1930's-something four-door DeSoto automobile, which sported a miniature human skull replica on the gear shifter! My brother and I, both of us mechanically minded (proven years later), greatly admired Grandpa's stick-shift skull. We delighted in watching it quiver when we sat in the car with the engine idling and the transmission out of gear. I believe it is very likely possible that the quivering stick-shift skull may have sometimes put us into a trance. Perhaps that's the reason Grandpa got the thing!

HOUSE NOISES AND DREAMS

I have very few specific recollections of my first year in school in Palmer Lake, Colorado. I do recall that I didn't like being away from Mom and Mike. But it seemed exciting, I think, to learn much more about numbers and letters. And Mike seemed always interested in and curious about what I was learning. The first house we lived in while in Palmer Lake was noisy and drafty and cold. I remember sometimes being frightened, especially when a strong wind was blowing at night when we were in bed and we could hear the house creak and groan. It seems Mike and I, on those nights, could quite clearly hear and imagine people walking around, maybe with crutches or a cane. Thump! Thump! Thump! Maybe a bear was inside the house somewhere! However, even worse were the seemingly frequent nightmares. I'm not sure of the cause of those vivid and frightening dreams, but they seemed almost always to involve bears and mountain lions and being chased by them. Those were my dreams. Mike, who became an avid outdoorsman, seemed to be rather unphased by my accounts of those nighttime images. But, at least, he never called me a "sissy!" So, I was never forced to "stop his clock" for a "time out."

COMIC BOOK CHARACTERS

Playing "Superman" and other comic book characters with Mike provided another kind of adventure for us. We proudly wore our "tea towel" capes as we "flew" off the tops of fence posts and porch railings! We worked very hard to find ways to extend our flight range with those "tea towel" capes a bit farther than three or four feet; but, sadly, to no avail. It seems, however, that we always "got our man" and justice always prevailed! Our comic book heroes were Batman, Captain Midnight, Superman and, of course, Dick Tracy. You'll find more information about "Dick Tracy" comic strips in Chapter 15.

SWEATERS AND SOCKS

My sense is that Mom was not working a paying job while in Palmer Lake. How we were able to live in the houses we occupied, I have no idea except that she must have been receiving some financial help. Her parents? Our father's parents? Someone else? I do not know any of that detail, and in later years it never occurred to me to ask about it. And, with three children to care for, how could Mom have ever held a job that would enable her to support the four of us – especially in a small town like Palmer Lake? Maybe she got some money from our father – although I doubt that. More likely, she received assistance from other family members. I don't know what kinds of help was available from "social services" kinds of outlets in those years, but I suspect it was nearly nothing if anything at all. But Mom could knit. I know that because I remember watching her knit sweaters and socks for us kids. I believe she made all, or nearly all, our clothes. She may have made things for other families who paid her for them. Of particular interest to me in those times was to watch Mom darn socks. What? Darn Socks? What, forevermore does that mean? Well, dear reader, if you don't know, then you are too young to remember back to the 1940s and 50s and before.

The first thing to understand is that nobody threw away a sock or stocking just because of a hole in it. It got repaired. Here's how. A specific tool or device was available to help with "darning socks," but because Mom probably could not afford the tool, she just used a simple smooth porcelain doorknob or maybe a trailer-hitch knob. Whether the hole in the sock was at the toe or the heel or elsewhere, apparently made no difference. She just placed the "knob" in the sock, stretched the affected area firmly over the knob and using her darning needle and yarn, made a woven repair in the affected area – in essence, weaving new material over the place of the hole in the sock. The doorknob helped "keep the shape" of the sock to ensure a better fit. This brings me back to working for income. It may well be that Mom "took in" damaged clothing items for repairs. Don't know. It's possible. Maybe she really did. Maybe she salted away a fortune in sock darning repair funds she never told anybody about! If someone happens to find that fortune, please inform the IRS. No, wait!! Inform me first, and I'll take care of informing those folks at the IRS, AFTER everything has been verified and all accounts settled and... well, you get the picture!

While it is difficult to recall specific things from ages five and six, I can however, bring to mind images of Mom's knitted and sewn sweaters, crafted shirts and light jackets and those darned socks! – maybe I should say, "those doggoned darned socks." Some of the colors she chose for sweaters, shirts and socks still stand out in my memory. I am relatively certain, thankfully, that she reserved pinks and pastels in wool and cotton fabrics, yarns and threads for our sister.

I'LL SHOW YOU MINE

This tale tells the story of the time of my first and only sort of private experience with a girl of my own age (or any age) before marriage! I do not remember her name or even what she looked like, except for her blond hair, but I apparently seemed to be attracted to her. Or, maybe it was that she was attracted to me. I don't know that I would have known the difference anyway. I probably wouldn't know the difference today either! But, I was a "first grader" that year! It was on one of our "playdays" when we were in a hay field out close to a horse barn, and quite far away from the house, playing hide-and-seek with several other kids. She and I had situated ourselves between a hay stack and a barbed-wire fence hiding from whomever was "it," when she spoke to me in a very quiet voice. She said, "I'll show you mine if you'll show me yours." I had no idea what she was talking about and that's what I said to her. So, she said something like, "Well, I'll just show you mine first, then." And she did! You can ask anybody who knew me as a teenager and even after high-school graduation, and many of those folks will comment about not ever knowing anyone as shy or as uninformed as Claude Romack about things sexual. Maybe that explains why I ran straight home without stopping after getting my first look at a girl's whatchamacallit. This revelation seems to beg the question: What ever happened to my supposed high level of curiosity?

Then came the lingering after-effects of that experience right after my marriage to Bonnie some decade and a half later. These mental images of the "behind the haystack" event seemed to somehow create a lot of skepticism and doubt on my part about the actual role of the male of a couple. It seems that questions began to arise in my mind about sexual aggressiveness (or lack of it) early on in our marriage. I think I can summarize my conclusion(s) by reflecting on comments by Dr. Norman Vincent Peale relative to "positive thinking." My takeaway from that reading was simply to let nature take its course and give it over to God. And some-place in this line of thinking are issues about respecting others and self-respect and simply doing what is right – personally, spiritually and sexually. As a further thought, and all due respect to my wonderful bride and long-time wife Bonnie, I'm not sure I looked on our wedding night, either! I think it was not a question of "where" I should look, but "whether" I should. At times like those, I believe that using one's imagination is sufficient, at least for a while, don't you?

A FIRE

At some later point, after seeing the girl's whatchamacallit, Mom moved us to a different house – not because of what I saw, but because of cheaper rent! It was a small kind of cottage, one on the edge of town at the bottom of a hill on a dirt road. This tiny little house had only three rooms, the living room serving also as a bedroom – or it may have been a bedroom serving as a living room. Heat was from a small wood/coal burning stove. The kitchen stove also used coal or wood. In today's real-estate circles, that little place would be marketed as a quaint, cute and rustic, but temporary, living accommodation. In those years, however, it was just a cheaper place for us.

My ever-adventurous brother was as bad about getting into mischief as I was at dealing with girls. He seemed to start out with a project that would somehow morph into a problem. On this occasion, his objective seemed to be getting rid of some fall leaves that collected in big piles on the little front porch of the little house where we had just moved. He got a bunch piled up about ten or twenty feet out in front of the house, close to the dirt road, got his box of matches (that he had hidden away from Mom), and lit a fire. I know. Some of you are wondering about "box of matches." What can I say? They were easier to use than flintstones to get a fire started! And they are now mostly just another part of our history. About half an hour later we had two fire trucks and several firemen around cleaning up after they got the fire put out. Very little damage was done to the little house. But it was close, they said, to becoming a real big problem. It is entirely possible that Mike found the whole experience very entertaining.

CHAPTER 3

Return to New Mexico

Ezekiel, Chapter 34, talks about Irresponsible Shepherds, and the True Shepherd, God being our True Shepherd. We are taught that God will look for us in our wandering and find us and lead us as does a good shepherd of sheep. We have but to follow Him, and God Himself will judge between the fat and the lean sheep.

Was Mom, at this point, inclined to wander? Was she searching? Was she confused and maybe distraught? By this time, our father having been "away" for possibly close to three years, was very likely not going to return. So, maybe it is that she was feeling and believing in directions from a higher power. It seems likely that Mom had possibly begun to turn to God.

BACK TO ALBUQUERQUE

I do not know the chronology here for sure, but it must have been something like this: sometime near the end of my first-grade schooling in Colorado Springs, everybody, meaning uncles Coy and Ward and the people of the racecar business, had, again, returned to Albuquerque. I believe Mom was compelled to make the move with them because she would, at least, have the comfort of being with members of her own biological family, specifically her brother and a sister. We all settled, it seems, within easy driving distance from one another, again, over in the northwest quadrant of Albuquerque, west of the Rio Grande river and with the familiar view of the dormant volcanos farther to the northwest. We had easy access to the sand and the sage brush and rattlesnakes - and sheep. At this point, and as stated earlier, it was clear that our father had left us. And, apparently, Mom had no idea where he was or what he was doing. Perhaps it was in his thinking that he wanted a partner who didn't want children. Maybe he just wanted not to be found since WWII was still going strong, but beginning to look like the possibility of an end being near, with Korea beginning to become louder. After the return to Albuquerque, Mom found work with a business machine company – I think it was a business machine dealer selling adding machines and typewriters. For you "youngsters" reading this, please understand that in those days adding machines and typewriters were "pieces of equipment" that weighed pounds, not ounces. All were considerably larger than a loaf of bread and were made mostly of steel, plastics, and aluminum. They made mechanical noises upon use and memory storage was entirely the responsibility of the typist to properly store a hard copy of the work in a filing cabinet. Today, I have three four-drawer filing cabinets in which is stored sixty years of data – all properly (more or less) categorized and filed in properly (more or less) labeled file folders. I remember the name "Remington" typewriters and other office equipment. Search "business machines of the 1940s" for more information. Then, if you are more interested, find one of those machines and try to actually use it. My older office equipment is securely tucked away in another desk that has a "pull out" shelf with springs that lets the user pull out the typewriter, raise it, and lock it in place for use. I doubt I can even find ribbon and ink for it now. Maybe I'll try someday. It is electric and therefore super easy to use. Just don't drop it on your foot! As a sidelight, in later years in my high-school typing class one of our class members was a girl with only one complete hand. Several of our class members questioned the wisdom, and perhaps need, of someone with only one hand learning to type. It seems that this girl became the best typist of our class. Her best speed, I think I remember, was something close to eighty words per minute. And that was, I believe, prior to electric typewriters!!

We lived, for a while, near our grandparents Plunkett and later with Uncle Coy and Aunt Neva in a garage apartment attached to or near their house. We were close to a small airfield and surrounded by more sagebrush, cactus and sand. And rattlesnakes. I seem also to remember fields of lava beds, being we were fairly close to those extinct volcanos farther out west. Uncle Coy had a son, Elton Coy, same age as Mike, and a daughter, Norma Lee, about five years older. Mike and cousin Coy attended first grade, and I second grade at the Old Armijo School in west Albuquerque.

THE WAVE-OFF

This garage living unit (apartment) was perhaps two or three hundred yards from one of a small airfield's perimeter fences. One time (and it in fact was just "one time"), having seen a movie or heard a story that included information about a person on the ground "waving off" an airplane, I decided I should try doing that. I guess I believed it should be lots of fun and maybe even powerful, to cause an airplane to circle around the airfield and not land – at least not right away. When it became clear after my first "wave-off" that I could indeed prevent an airplane from landing, I tried it again after the plane circled around for another landing attempt. I waved him off again, successfully, and then I went home. A short time later, maybe two or three days, a man accompanied by "a person of authority" – he showed us a badge - visited us to ask if we knew of or had seen anybody a few days before at the end of the runway "waving" to incoming airplanes. I guess I thought I was going to get a compliment, or maybe even a gift, and responded right away with enthusiasm when I said something like "It was me! It was me!" My reward was a paddling and restriction from the end of the runway. I may have been put on a "bread and water" diet for a few days as well, which possibly explains why I never grew very tall since I seemed to be in trouble, perhaps more often than not.

CRUNCHY LUNCH

This little snippet is a bit gross, so choose now whether to read it. If you choose to read it, just understand you have been warned, fairly and squarely! If you begin to get "queasy," please stop reading. Need I comment further? Mike and I, remembering our former exposure to living among the sage brush, cactus, tumbleweeds, sand, lava beds, and whatever else one finds in this high desert country, were glad to get back into an environment we "sorta" understood. Thus, it was with that mindset early on one sunny morning when the weather was cooling a bit, we decided on a little foray into the open land to our north and west. Best I recall, we decided to not pack anything to eat, or maybe it was that Mom admonished us to return in an hour or so. In either case it meant we carried nothing with us to eat. We did take a canteen of water, however. Note: One of our usual instructions about being out among the cactus and sagebrush was to be back well before dark. For it is that in the late afternoons around dusk that the snakes and other desert wildlife are out looking for supper. We also took a paper bag just in case we might need one, I guess. You can never tell what might be found in the high desert country that one would wish to bring back. Things like unusual rocks or snake or rabbit skeletons. If it was springtime instead of fall and we found a fresh new cactus with a blossom, Mom would be pleased.   When the hunger pangs inevitably started, we did a search for something to eat. You know how it is with young kids, don't you? It takes only a nanosecond to experience hunger. Note: I think we didn't use the term "nanosecond" then, but I'm comfortable using it here. Continuing: That's what happened to us. We got hungry right away, it seems. Since we carried nothing with us to eat, we decided to "improvise." We didn't use that word either, of course, but you know what I mean here. Right? Here's kind of the way it went. Sagebrush, in the fall, is dull and lackluster and uninviting. The grass has begun to dry and turn brown. No pine nut trees, thus no pine nuts around either. (I don't have the right keyboard to write pin-yone properly – so you get pine nuts!) We did, however, find, in clusters, little gatherings of small pecan sized "things" that seemed okay, but required a sip of water with each bite. We found that we liked them so much, we filled our paper sack about half full of them in order to have some when we got back to the house. They were dry and a little "crunchy," but with a sort of obscure non-identifiable taste – kind of neutral, I guess.

On the way home, each time we found one of those clusters, we'd eat two or three and put some more in the bag. By the time we arrived home, we were full, so was the bag! We were so happy to be able to tell Mom we wouldn't be needing supper, we could hardly contain ourselves. And we proudly explained and showed to Mom the results of our exploration and foraging skills. Oh, yes. One thing I "forgot" to mention earlier was the presence of quite a number of sheep in that same area. Just thought you should know that!

Knowing what I know now, having experienced several years ago some severe incidents related to a dysfunction in my now older intestinal system, what Mom made Mike and me do immediately on returning home was the exact and proper and safe thing to do. She made us drink water until we thought we were about to explode. And then, drink some more! Eventually, we had taken in enough water that added to that which we had eaten, we had no choice but to "upchuck" probably about all that we had eaten. It could have been that Mom stuck a long finger down each throat to help that process. Probably, however, it wasn't long before we were ready again for something to eat! You know how most kids are, don't you? – Always hungry! That was us.

ALONE AND CONFUSED

Later, Mom found a place not too remote from the rest of the family but closer in toward downtown, not far off old Highway 66, and much closer to her workplace. For us two boys, it was a short walk to school, and we were closer to the river. In retrospect this was a time of confusion. Both of us boys were often left by ourselves – especially after Mom started dating. And for the life of me, I cannot seem to recall Mary's disposition except to say that Sis was likely either living with or taken each workday to be with our maternal grandparents.

I have little or no significant recollection of that second year of school at the Old Armijo School in west Albuquerque where the grounds were 100 percent sand – more about this in Chapter 7. I know we walked to and from the school. I remember being admonished to not even walk in the direction of the river from the school. (That would be the Rio Grande River whose banks in that area would not have been very far from the school – possibly less than a mile.) Except for the grounds and the walking to and from the school I have no other memories pertaining to my second year of public education. I do recall seeing small desert animals, mostly rabbits, squirrels, and chipmunks on my walks to and from school.

INTRODUCING X, SORT OF

First is to explain the use of "X." It is a simple matter of my refusal to honor him with the use of his given name. Second, he is deceased, so it is not about revealing something to which he might object. Third, knowing his name would neither add to nor subtract from this accounting. Fourth, family and close friends will easily know to whom I refer. Fifth, both of my sisters as well as my wife agree with me, and that's the acid test! My most significant memory group of that time is the lonely and quiet times after school waiting for Mom to get home. She had started dating sometime during that year, but I do not recall ever meeting anyone until the first time she had X with her. And I remember seeing him only once before Mike and I were on our way to Oklahoma at the end of the school year. As I visualize that scene at this moment, the image is of a well-groomed, well dressed pleasant looking man with dark wavy (almost curly) hair and who exhibited a nice smile. I describe his general appearance as firmly built, sort of stocky and with a healthy appearance. If he spoke to either Mike or me, I cannot recall. But it seems he exhibited a friendly demeanor.

It was not long after that meeting and after school session was over, when Uncle Charlie showed up one day and loaded Mike, Mary, and me with all our "stuff" into his car and took us to Pawnee, Oklahoma. By this time, our father had been gone for more than three years, and it seems certain that Mom was likely quite desperate for a better life. But, that's not how it was to be for more than a decade. On our arrival in Pawnee, probably two or three days after leaving Albuquerque, Mary Sue, age-five, was settled in with grandparents Plunkett, while my brother and I got a room all to ourselves in Uncle Charlie and Aunt Alma's house. Mike attended second grade and I third grade in Pawnee during our stay with this wonderful aunt and uncle during parts of 1948 and 1949.

CHAPTER 4

Aunt Alma and Uncle Charlie

The memory of the righteous is blessed,
but the name of the wicked will rot.
Proverbs 10:7 (NKJV)

The little town of Pawnee, Oklahoma is very close to my heart because it is the place of my meeting of and marriage to my precious life mate Bonnie, my high school graduation, and much of my early work life. But it was through this incredible period of fifteen or sixteen months with Aunt Alma and Uncle Charlie that Mike and I received our introduction to Pawnee. Consequently, even though Pawnee is a place of many family related trials and tribulations, as alluded to previously, it is also a place of numerous good events and accomplishments and memories. Pawnee reappears in this writing again in Chapter 13 – Leaving and Arriving. [Chapter 4 deals with Mike and me living with Aunt Alma and Uncle Charlie in parts of '48 & '49, grade 2 for Mike and grade 3 for me. Mary, at age five, lived with grandparents Plunkett.] About a year after completion of this visit, we moved to the sawmill site in New Mexico.

Other than my marriage to Bonnie and the births of our sons, living with Aunt Alma and Uncle Charlie is among the highest of highlights in my life, thus my blessed memory of the righteous. Discussion of the "wicked" begins in Chapter 5.

MY FAVORITE AUNT AND UNCLE

Aunt Alma was quiet and gentle, although sometimes calculating and bossy. But my impressions of her after the first few weeks of living in her house included learning that she seemed to never sit still for more than a few moments. She smiled a lot and seemed always to have something pleasant to talk about. Mike and I, after a short period of time in her house, came to believe that Aunt Alma must have also performed house "chores" in her sleep. Amazing woman!

Uncle Charlie was a "man's man." He was a man of many "work" talents. He chain-smoked unfiltered cigarettes (Wings). He could tear down and rebuild a truck engine, he moved houses; he collected and sold scrap iron during WWII to help in the war effort. He almost always smelled of sweat, smoke, grease, oil, and gasoline and whatever animal he had last petted or hunted. For recreation, food and pelts, he hunted rabbit, fox, coon, opossum, and deer – and he never came home empty handed. He was the only <u>real</u> "father figure" Mike and I ever experienced until well into our adulthood years when Mom married Dick Hinds (whom we "kids" nicknamed "Pappy"). This "visit" with Uncle Charlie and Aunt Alma lasted for a little more than fifteen wonderful months starting in mid-Spring, 1948, and ending in late Summer, 1949.

I'm interrupting the flow here for a moment or two to elaborate on Wings Cigarettes. In my research to establish correctness of brand name and other items concerning the cigarettes, I discovered something I wish I had known back in 1948 and 49, namely that the cigarette brand sponsored quite an array of "Wings Airplane" cards (collector's cards). Perhaps I'll take an interest in doing such collecting, although, after a brief bit of research, it appears the effort would be relatively expensive at this point. Wings brand cigarettes are still popular, presumably because they are still cheaper than other brands. And it also appears that Wings has a strong following of card collectors. The cigarettes were introduced in 1929 and sold for ten cents per pack compared to other brands selling for 25 cents per two packs. That would explain why Uncle Charlie preferred Wings. Perhaps this subject will lead to another story of sorts. We'll see!

Following those fifteen or so months in Pawnee plus nearly another year in Albuquerque, we found ourselves moving into the northwest mountains of New Mexico to a sawmill site at Iron Spring canyon inside the far western (and smallest) section of Carson National Forest. Separating this western portion of Carson NF from the eastern sections is the Continental Divide and the Jicarilla Apache Indian Reservation. Chapter 8 contains the beginning of that part of this story.

ABOUT MARY

Mary had just reached her fifth birthday at the beginning of our stay in Pawnee. Mom sent her with Mike and me when Uncle Charlie arrived in Albuquerque to pick us up, but Mary lived with our grandparents Plunkett while Mike and I lived with Aunt Alma and Uncle Charlie. It seems quite likely that Mom believed she needed some "space" to regain some focus or maybe some normalcy in her life following the desertion of our biological father; but also, her new relationship with X. Also, highly likely would have been serious financial issues for her.

For reasons unfathomable to me, I recollect no interaction among the three of us kids during those approximately fifteen months in Pawnee.

Those months held many adventures and exciting times for Mike and me that seemed to neither permit nor encourage activities elsewhere or otherwise. And now that I think more deeply about it, an explanation and/or apology for/to Mary seems to be in order here. So, Sis, please accept my slightly late apology (on behalf of Mike too) for this gross oversight of ours in 1947 and 48. We really didn't mean to ignore you! By that I mean our minds and interests just seemed to be much more focused on dogs and rifles and shotguns and hunting and "helping" Aunt Alma and Uncle Charlie and looking after Grandma Topper. I guess you could call it "guy stuff." Incidentally, just for thoroughness and clarity, please know that I will soon verbally express this same apology to Sis. She deserves it. So, please help me remember to do so! I'm counting on you, for my memory (recent) function seems more and more to falter and stumble!

OUR PAWNEE "PARENTS"

Early in April 1947 Uncle Charlie showed up in Albuquerque where Mom, Mike, Mary, and I were living in a garage apartment next to or attached to the residence of Mom's brother, Coy and his wife Neva and their two children, Elton Coy and Norma Lee. Probably two or three days later, Mike, Mary, and I, with Uncle Charlie were in Pawnee, Oklahoma, at his house on West Harrison Street, also known as Highway 64. Those approximately fifteen months we had with Uncle Charlie and Aunt Alma included our attending a full year of school in Pawnee. My third-grade teacher was Mrs. Teague who, a few years later, became our next-door neighbor when we relocated to Pawnee. Also, as a point of interest, Mrs. Teague's husband (Ralph) was the high school shop teacher, and it was in taking his class a few years later that I developed a keen interest in woodworking. Thus, my garage has been taken over by woodworking equipment and tools! And I still have in my possession a table lamp of birds-eye maple and black walnut that is today part of our dinette area furnishings. It was one of my wood-shop projects in the 1955-56 school year.

It seems the first thing that became obvious to us two boys was that Aunt Alma and Uncle Charlie were quiet and gentle. No slaps, no yelling, no obvious anger. We had a bath each night and clean clothes every day. And Aunt Alma always made sure we got enough to eat. Their two daughters, Arleta and Quilladean, were both away from home and working or in college. Uncle Charlie's mother – whom we knew as Mrs. Topper or Grandma Topper lived in the house also.

The house was a sort of rambling structure with an inviting front entry, although not a large one. The front door entered directly into a quite large living room that immediately reflected a place of quiet living with neat and comfortable furniture. Mike and I were assigned to the side bedroom, a room right off the dining room, with large windows on the east side looking out onto a very large and grassy yard that extended northward toward a small barn that sheltered several rabbit hutches. I first, then Mike suffered through both measles and chicken pox in that bedroom. Two other bedrooms and a very large enclosed back porch just off the kitchen completed the layout.

The entire property consisted of probably two acres of land with a large shop, the rabbit pens, a small barn, and a quite large metal building full of workbenches and tools and space for two or three vehicles. Outside the house, in addition to all the work-related structures and space, was a giant pecan tree under which we hand-cranked several different batches of ice cream through both summers. I, two or three years later, confirmed in somewhat nefarious ways that my brother and I had been farmed out to Uncle Charlie and Aunt Alma and Mary to grandparents Plunkett, as a matter of convenience for the relationship between Mom and X, whom you'll learn much more about in Chapter 5.

First Photograph At Age 10 Months With Uncle Charlie

Another item connected with my "Pawnee Parents" came to me just a few days ago. It was the photograph above of Uncle Charlie holding me, in front of his Auto Parts store/shop next door to his house, probably a few days prior to April 18, 1940. An accompanying photo (which I do not have permission to include) shows a black woman, whose name is/was Opal H., holding me. The note on the back reveals that it was taken also in April 1940. That it was taken in Pawnee is not certain. Along with these photographs is a note written by Mom in pencil on April 19, 1940 on note paper with letterhead announcing Oneal (no apostrophe) Hotel, Dodge City, Kansas. The letterhead also includes the hotel ownership names and nightly room rates of "$1.00 and up." The message Mom wrote reads: "Ellis's (my middle name) first night in a hotel. We were on our way from Pawnee, Oklahoma to Palmer Lake, Colorado." Mom also wrote that we met with Coy (her brother) on April 20, after staying at the Oneal Hotel the night before. But, for the life of me, I do not recall that meeting.

In the same envelope with the pictures and hotel stationary note is a small Birth Announcement card revealing my full name, Claude Ellison Romack, which is proof enough for me that I was named after my two grandfathers: Claude Romack and Ellison Plunkett; Ellison being the formal rendition of Ellis. In that same group of photographs was the image shown below of Uncle Charlie and Aunt Alma in their "Sunday Best" seated in their living room, possibly having just returned home from church, but more likely from some formal gathering in town since Uncle Charlie seldom, if ever, attended church. I call your attention also to the shelves behind Uncle Charlie. I clearly remember that Mike and I both admired all of those display items. However, we were not allowed to remove them from the shelves. We could look and touch, but not remove them. This photograph was taken in late 1950 or early 1951.

Charles and Alma Topper circa 1950 – 51

GRANDMA TOPPER

If I had felt the need to create a nickname or moniker for Grandma Topper, it would have been something like "snoop" or "eagle eye" or, maybe, "tattletale." Mike and I both agreed that it was because of Grandma Topper that Aunt Alma seemed to always know what and when we were doing things questionable or not allowed at all. Once we became aware of that news source for Aunt Alma, it seems to have become a "game" between us boys and Grandma Topper for the remainder of our time in Pawnee.

Grandma Topper always sat for her meals at the dining room table across from the west windows of the dining room. A large bureau, with the radio setting on it, was behind her. To a boy at age nine, she looked ancient. She must have been, I remember thinking, at least sixty-five years old! And she smoked! She "rolled her own," not believing in "store bought" cigarettes. She loved listening to news reports from John Cameron Swayze.

She said she liked his firm and sincere voice and his presentation, whatever that meant! When she had her breakfast, she used fresh-brewed coffee instead of milk on her cereal because milk was "for youngsters like you," she would say, with a "put on" scowl toward Mike and me.

Her clear gray eyes, hook nose, and tiny mouth seemed to cause her to look formidable. But she talked in a voice that was barely above a whisper. If she got louder than that you had ample reason to suspect the person she was addressing was in trouble! And, of course, that person was generally Mike or me. I think she believed her son, Uncle Charlie, to be a saint and I say that with admiration. If memory serves, Grandma Topper lived to be a little over ninety years of age which was really something in the 1950s. She was born just prior to the beginning of the Civil War and President Abraham Lincoln's time in office.

UNCLE CHARLIE, A MAN'S MAN

When I think of Uncle Charlie, my thoughts almost always go directly to visualizing him as my "real" father. I didn't realize the significance then of his quiet and confident example of living, working and laughing. He and Aunt Alma raised two daughters, who both achieved college degrees. Mike and I were privileged to have been under the quiet and confident care of this aunt and uncle for that one year-and-a-quarter in 1947 and 1948. It was sometime in that period that Mom married X, which confirms, to some degree, my belief that Mike and I were "sent" to live with Aunt Alma and Uncle Charlie for convenience.

But regardless of the reason, we two boys never received an explanation. On the other hand, we could not have received a better experience than living over a year with Aunt Alma and Uncle Charlie! Also, regardless of the reason, our time with them was the only direct example we ever had and shared, before adulthood, of real fatherhood. I have, since that time, always thought of Uncle Charlie as the absolute best example of a loving, caring, and devoted father to two young boys. Uncle Charlie was, for me, an outstanding example of a "family man." He was kind, loving, industrious, forward looking and considerate to the nth degree toward all around him, and he was always fair. Although he didn't participate in any church activities, he never used foul language, and he didn't scream or yell or even raise his voice. And he was generous with both his time and money.

My other two "Pawnee" uncles were Coy and Ward. Ward, the husband of my mother's sister, Myrtle, was comparable to Uncle Charlie in many ways, i.e., great work ethic, accommodating, and friendly. His primary business was hiring out his bulldozer and related mechanical "tools" to build ponds, terraces, and other dirt moving chores, mostly in Pawnee county. Coy, mom's brother, served in WWII as a Navy Machinists Mate. He was soft spoken and always considerate. His work, after the war, was as a mechanic for the Chrysler/Dodge/Plymouth dealer in Tulsa. It was Uncle Coy's example that inspired me to join the U.S. Navy. So, it's easy for me to confirm that all three of these uncles could be referred to as "Men's Men." My siblings and I learned later, much to our disappointment and chagrin, few, if any, similarities in familial relationships existed between these uncles and X.

AUNT ALMA, KINDNESS PERSONIFIED

Some might describe her (these days) as "Mrs. Clean." Others might lean toward "quietly industrious." I believe I could go through an entire dictionary or other kinds of word sources and find dozens of words and/or terms that would describe Aunt Alma in very kind and even eloquent ways. As with Uncle Charlie, I never witnessed raised voice, anger, temper fits, or any other negative or aggressive expressions or conditions or behavior in Aunt Alma. If I attempted to describe all her attributes that I know about, you'd be reading for quite a while longer in this section. Instead, I will comment about traits like her sense of humor, her sincerity, and her faith as I witnessed them a few years later when we relocated to Pawnee from the sawmill near the beginning of Fall, 1951, when I entered the sixth grade. But I was old enough and knowledgeable enough to appreciate the woman who was my Aunt Alma.

Aunt Alma's sense of humor would have been described by many as "guarded." She would never laugh at someone else's expense, except (perhaps) if that person was laughing also, but maybe not even then. That, in my estimation, indicates a high degree of self-discipline and careful consideration. One thing about her laughter, however, was its contagiousness. Once she started, those near her would "get the bug" and join in. I believe this happened mostly because of her giggly and squeaky kind of laugh that seemed to compel anyone else within hearing distance to join in. Most who knew her would agree that when Aunt Alma was expressing something in sincere tones, she was indeed being sincere. It was never an act.

I believe that for her to speak in "sincere" tones and not be sincere was not possible, as well. For her to behave in an insincere way I think was simply not possible.

I do not recall ever attending church with Aunt Alma in those years. In fact, I'm not sure she even went to church when Mike and I lived with them during my third-grade year and Mike's second-grade year. But she read her Bible. And not just on Sundays – I believe it was most evenings before going to bed that she would read for about an hour. I think I was terrified that at some point she was going to ask me to give the blessing over a meal. Uncle Charlie sometimes would, but it seems that was something she liked doing herself most of the time. I'm sure she's doing just fine in heaven. She likely has things under control and everything in its place and she has lots of friends. God probably immediately placed Aunt Alma in charge of very important things having to do with cleanliness of mind, body and soul!

A SPECIAL KIND OF REARING

Following are some bits 'n pieces of information about the kind of "rearing" Aunt Alma and Uncle Charlie provided for us. The base information about Uncle Charlie is that he never had a "job" per se'; meaning he never "worked for wages," that I know about. It seems he just gravitated from one thing to another doing whatever looked promising enough to create some income. If he ever had a "work portfolio," it would have contained more than a few pages. I believe he had no concept of the idea of not working. During WW II one of his businesses was collecting and selling scrap metal (as alluded to earlier) which, along with his age, kept him out of the military during WWII, and later, Korea. (I'm not sure, but I believe Uncle Charlie was above the age limit for the military draft for WWII.) His biggest and best customer was, then, the USA. He gravitated to moving houses following WWII, and along the way, he somehow developed an interest in raising rabbits.

It was during this time that he drove to New Mexico and brought Mike, Mary, and me to Pawnee. Now, whenever we are in Pawnee, I drive by the location where Uncle Charlie had his property until the mid-1970s: his rabbit pens and dog pens, his mountains of scrap iron during WWII and Korea, the giant pecan tree in the front yard, and the always very neat house that Aunt Alma was so proud of. At this writing all those buildings, fences, and trees are gone and, as of a few weeks ago, some new construction has started. I think of the good times Mike and I had in that house and on the scrap-iron pile and in the garage shop and on the roof of the barn and in the barn come breeding time for the rabbits, and the tomato juice bath – I'll tell you more about those items along with some others, starting now.

THE MATING OF BUCKS AND DOES

One of the first things Uncle Charlie did on our arrival in Pawnee was to introduce Mike and me to his hound dogs that he used for opossum and coon hunting, then he showed us his rabbit pens and feed storage. Sometime soon after those exposures, it came time for him to supervise the mating of the bucks and does. If you're not familiar with the mating of rabbits in a commercial setting, here's a very brief explanation: When it is determined that a doe is in "heat," a buck is placed with her in her pen and they mate. The mating process is quite fast, so you must "watch close the first time," so to speak. Stated another way, when the buck has determined the doe is in heat, he mounts her and very quickly the "deed is done." Most of us would probably consider the act of rabbits mating as very aggressive or maybe even violent. Writing this reminds me of Ray Stevens' "Don't Look Ethyl!" song because of the "job" Uncle Charlie assigned to Mike and me, during breeding time.

This "job," when Uncle Charlie had Mike and me helping him, was to serve as lookouts. One of us would be at the rabbit hutch area and the other up close to the back door of the house. With a prearranged signal whichever of us was by the back door of the house was to signal the other at the rabbit hutches if Aunt Alma was coming outside. The explanation for this activity when one of us asked "why?" was simple. Uncle Charlie very directly looked at us and said quietly, (imagine this in a quiet Ronald Reagan voice) "Well, your Aunt Alma is a very kind and gentle woman, and she just ought not see this." At ages seven and eight, Mike and I had neither the presence of mind nor the benefits of other similar experiences, to ask "why."

By the time of our high school years in Pawnee just a few years later, Mike and I had frequent visits with Aunt Alma and Uncle Charlie. We learned much more about our open and articulate and genuine and genteel and gracious Aunt Alma. We needed no further information then to understand Uncle Charlie's concern, those several years earlier out by the rabbit pens about being "on the lookout" for Aunt Alma.

CHAIN-LINK FENCE AND CEMENT MIXER

Probably because of some city ordinance, Uncle Charlie was required to have a specific type of fence around some parts of his property because of his scrap-iron piles, rabbit hutches, chicken house, and large garage building for his truck maintenance as well as the parking area for his trucks and housing for his hunting dogs. This six-foot tall fence was of chain-link and steel post construction, and it surrounded a very large area. His barn structure, or more accurately "shop" as I recall, was on the extreme west end of his property, close against a side road going north that eventually crossed the railroad tracks. Another structure, the hen house, or maybe it was the old barn, had a roof of corrugated sheet metal that had only a moderate slope, so being on top of it was not particularly difficult. However, it was slippery when wet. It was on one of those damp days when Mike and I decided we should climb up on that roof. So, we did.

Now, this structure was close to part of a chain-link fence that ran parallel to the length of the sloped roof. I was then, and am today, rather awkward and clumsy at some things. Playing sports, for instance, is not and was not in my field of competency – not even close! That morning after Mike and I had gotten up on the hen house roof we went all the way to the top so we could see all around. We looked. We saw. And on the way down, I slipped and slid down the roof toward that chain-link fence. Mike told me later, after Aunt Alma applied a bunch of bandages, that I looked "real neat" sliding down and off that roof.

The thing about chain-link fencing material is that the top and bottom edges are made up of the ends of the heavy large-gauge wire that creates the fencing. And they have sharp points. I fell on top of those, so that was where I got those scars on my chest that are now about four inches apart and from shoulder to shoulder. They are each about three inches long now but have faded away quite a bit. After all, it's only been a little over seventy years since that mishap! (By the way, my seventy-ninth birthday was just yesterday!!) Three of the scars are still visible, but I believe I started with five. I don't know for sure. It is highly likely that two of those five scars got covered up with surgical scars since I've had so many surgeries.

Aunt Alma expressed shock; Uncle Charlie laughed. It was a month or two later when I decided to see if I could rotate the drum of the cement mixer Uncle Charlie kept in the west side yard. At first, it was difficult. The mixer had been setting unused for quite a while, I guess, so it was hard to turn the drum. I found a can of oil in the barn and decided some lubrication would help me to turn that drum. It worked. But I was turning it "by hand," i.e., without operating the small gasoline engine. To do it by hand required gripping the cogs on the drum to get it turning. On about my second or third pull I didn't get my hand out of the way fast enough and the middle finger of my right hand got pulled in between the cogs on the drum and the cogged drive wheel.

That scar is still visible also. And the finger is a little crooked as well – I think from some arthritis. But, I can still type, and at this exact moment, that's a very good thing! Aunt Alma didn't seem too surprised. Uncle Charlie just wore a smile that expressed resigned pity. So, this then was, for two little boys, the illustration and example of the heart and mind of a man who obviously loved and adored and respected his wife: a woman capable of giggling and being compassionate at the same time. In retrospect, it seems that responses like those from Aunt Alma and Uncle Charlie were unexpected by Mike and me.

A TOMATO JUICE BATH

Have you ever eaten opossum or raccoon meat? If not, don't! If you have, then you already know not to do it again – except in dire emergency. Several times Mike and I accompanied Uncle Charlie, and sometimes one or two other men, on raccoon and opossum hunts with their dogs. I believe these were really raccoon hunts only, but somehow hunters usually also ended up with an opossum or two. Maybe it was that the opossums became dog food, which would be a good thing. The reason for the special interest in raccoons was the appeal and value of their pelts and, particularly, their tails. A "must have" for a young man in those years, was a raccoon tail flying from his car radio antenna.

One of those nights, things went just flat-out wrong! Not long after the hunt started, the dogs discovered a large group of skunks; I guess a family of them. So, it was, that we all came home completely covered in skunk odor. The root cause was that the dogs had to be rescued from the skunks! So, not only did we have skunk odor transfer from the dogs, but directly from the skunks themselves! This was when we discovered the truth about whether soap and water will remove skunk odor. Then we tried bathing in kerosene. But when Mike and I showed up for school (Actually, I think the hunt was on a Saturday evening, and we spent Sunday trying to rid ourselves of the skunk odor,) Mrs. Teague, my third-grade teacher, swatted me on the rear while she held her nose and sent me home. Mike received the same treatment from his teacher.

To my knowledge, none of us guys counted the cans of tomato juice, but my guess is somewhere in the seventy-five to eighty range – about twenty gallons. Those were the large cans that contained something like thirty-two ounces. Why tomato juice? Someone had said the skunk odor could be removed by bathing in it. So, Uncle Charlie, Mike, and I spent parts of the next three days in the backyard bathing and soaking in tomato juice by using a galvanized wash tub and taking turns. Uncle Charlie was not a large man, but he still had difficulty fitting into the wash tub. Oh, what I wouldn't give to have photographs, in color, of that event! Mike and I thought it was funny. Uncle Charlie didn't! That's also when Mike and I learned more about Aunt Alma's squeaky laugh which pierced our ears as she watched us three near-naked guys in the backyard taking tomato juice baths in that galvanized wash tub! And it was nice getting a break from school – maybe as a reward? Maybe not. We got to eat and sleep in the backyard too! It was a very memorable adventure for two kids. Uncle Charlie has probably shared that story with God by now, likely more than once!

THE GRANDDADDY RACCOON

Uncle Charlie's style of dealing with us boys was direct. He always "called a spade a spade." He didn't pull punches. He didn't lie or make up stories. The event I am relating to you now became sort of a "life lesson" for Mike and me, and it was something we talked about years later, almost with reverence. This story depicts some animal violence, so beware! This event did in fact happen. I'm hoping my recap of it is at least relatively accurate in the finer detail. But the event, as I relate it here, was factual in scope if not in detail. Occasionally, many of the hunters with hunting dogs, and more specifically "coon" dogs, would gather at an agreed-upon location out of town and bring along some horses and their dogs. They convened for one of these gatherings when someone of their group had captured and kept alive a large (usually male) raccoon. For this gathering, the captured raccoon was particularly large – among the largest they had ever had, someone opined. In fact, its weight would likely have been nearly equal to that of some of the smaller dogs. The starting place would always be near a body of water. The raccoon would have already been transported to the area inside multilayered gunny sacks tied shut with rope. When everyone was ready, the sacked raccoon was dunked in water, and then dragged along the "trail" through the woods by horse to a previously specified area and turned loose and made to climb into an already selected large and tall tree. When all that was accomplished, a pistol was fired to signal those back at the beginning point that the "hunt" was on. Someone stayed near the tree to make sure the raccoon remained in place.

Uncle Charlie rarely entered any of his dogs into these events, but he often liked to attend this "hunt" just to see other dogs and for friendship with other hunters. I believe he had no entries on this occasion, but he may have. Here is how I remember this event: Three dogs, all belonging to one man, were the first to reach the tree where the raccoon was "treed." One of the dogs that was a "tree climber" proceeded to climb. When the dog reached the raccoon, the result was that both fell out of the tree, the raccoon had the dog by the throat and the dog was dead or dying. This event worsened dramatically as this very large raccoon attacked and killed the other two dogs. And the raccoon escaped!

Uncle Charlie was extremely upset by this event. I believe he never attended another. He was upset by the loss of the dogs, of course, but also because he had exposed both of us boys to this bloody, gory, and violent event. He spent hours and hours with us separately and together over the remaining time we had with him and Aunt Alma. His apologies seemed endless and during one of our discussions, he cried. Not bawling, but with a strained voice and tears streaming down his face. And he made it clear to us boys that the apology was for subjecting us to such violence, even though it was "just" some dogs.

AUNT ALMA'S BRASSIERES

Where Aunt Alma and Uncle Charlie had gone, I do not know. I did know they were not home but would be back in "a while," the note on the door said. The thing is, we didn't know when they had left for their venture. Mike and I had just gotten home from school. Thus, we had the house to ourselves since Grandma Topper had gone with Aunt Alma and Uncle Charlie, so she could "get some sun." Like many homes of the time, the house (which no longer exists) on West Harrison in Pawnee sported a back bathroom that also was part of the enclosed back porch, and as such, included a laundry area and some closets and an indoor clothes line that ran the length of the room. Also, at the west end of the room was an outside door giving easy access to the barn, rabbit hutches, and dog pens. When Aunt Alma had only a small collection of just-laundered items, she usually hung them on her indoor line on the back porch. Not many things were hung to dry and I do not remember what the other pieces were, but I do remember that several of Aunt Alma's brassieres were on the line (she would not have hung those articles outdoors anyway). We two young guys spotted the "under things" and were apparently attracted to them for some then unknown reason. We snatched down one apiece and because we had decided we would "model" them, we proceeded to do so. Therefore, we must have known what they were used for and that they were something Uncle Charlie would have probably not ever considered handling himself.

Uncle Charlie kept his vehicles in good repair, so other than engine sounds or tires crunching on gravel, noise from them was rare. Such was the circumstance when they returned from their "in-town" venture. Mike and I never heard the car nor the opening and closing of the car doors. No horn was honked announcing their arrival either. I guess we also didn't hear the front door of the house open because we were so engrossed in admiring ourselves in a mirror. This was when we got caught with "our pants down" so to speak. We did have our jeans on, but our torsos were bare – except for the brassieres. Mike and I were just skinny little kids so we had to tie knots in the straps. Aunt Alma didn't like what she saw, not one bit! And she made sure we knew of her displeasure.

I remember Aunt Alma directing Uncle Charlie to "switch" each of us "just one time" and he could do that while she took her brassieres to the laundry room to be untangled and rewashed. I believe we were not old enough to be embarrassed, but we sure didn't like getting punished for something we were having fun doing, even though it was only "one switch" apiece. But the best of this memory was hearing Uncle Charlie's throaty, but contained, laugh and Aunt Alma's squeaky (tee-hee-hee) giggle as they were preparing for bed that night. I think it is possible, but not likely, that they were amused about something else.

COUSINS, BICYCLES, AND "COWBOYS AND INDIANS"

One of the nice benefits of having lived with Aunt Alma and Uncle Charlie was that we had access to all our cousins since they all lived in Pawnee at that time. Among Mom and her two sisters and one brother, were eleven offspring – six girls and five boys. The three oldest of us were girls. I was the oldest of the boys. Of the three younger girls, two are my sisters, Mary and Donna. Of the five boys, three achieved college degrees, my brother and I did not. The girls were split three and three for collegiate achievement. At this writing three of the five male cousins are still living. My brother died in 1997 and my cousin Roy died early in 2017. The years '47 and '48 seem, in many ways, to have been pivotal for Mike and me primarily because of our first and greatest exposure to a "father" figure in Uncle Charlie (as mentioned earlier). At that time, we were unaware of the entrance of X into our lives. It was also during this time in Pawnee - a little over a full year – that Mike and I got our first bicycles. Uncle Charlie had bought two of them at an auction for five dollars apiece – a tidy sum in 1947. Mine was sort of blue-green and Mike's was red. Each bike had a chain guard and "real-rubber" hand grips. Uncle Charlie tutored us on how best to take care of these bikes as well as the necessity to do so. I have no knowledge of what the girl cousins did when they got together. Not one of us male cousins was "tuned in" to girls yet anyway.

But memory is quite clear about what we boys did. We played Cowboys and Indians. Many movies of the time were featuring such people as Tom Mix, Roy Rogers, Gene Autry, Lash Larue, The Lone Ranger and Tonto, to name just a few. Among us boys were my brother Mike, cousins Elton Coy (Coy), Roy, and Roy's younger brother Tom (we tried to get him to not participate because of his age and size.), and me – the oldest of the boys. Now my being the oldest, one would think, would put me in charge. Roy, on the other hand, seemed to be the tallest, at least in his eyes. Not only that, his name was ROY. None of the rest of us had the name of a popular movie star except for Tom, but being the youngest, he didn't count even though western star Tom Mix was no "lightweight" in the movie industry then either. But Roy Rogers was advertised as "King of the Cowboys" and remained so for many years. So that automatically put ROY in charge.

Well, so much for that argument. Claude Akins had come on the movie scene by then, but he was not a major movie star as he later became – and that was too late for me. Besides, what serious cowboy "fan" would ever choose to use the name "Claude" while playing "Cowboys & Indians"? My given name was never used among us cousins or by aunts and uncles or even grandparents. My nickname "Pinky" was given me at birth by one of the delivery room nurses as you read in Chapter One. Pinky Lee, the entertainer, wasn't very popular over the radio, and we were years away from television at that time. He (Pinky Lee) never appeared, to my knowledge, in western or cops 'n robbers movies anyway. So, leadership as a result of having a "famous" name, on my part, was out of the question. Those were the good ole' days! I'm not now and wasn't then much of a star fan anyway. Many "stars," at least in their own minds, seem to have self-elevated their societal importance to unrealistic and unearned levels.

ARLETA AND QUILLADEAN

These two women are/were the oldest of this generation of "cousins" and were the offspring of Aunt Alma and Uncle Charlie. Arleta's husband, Melburn, was deployed with the U.S. Army to Korea during that war. I have heard (but never confirmed) that Melburn piloted landing craft in Korea – a truly dangerous job. I am unaware of any specific military decorations he most likely received. He returned from the war and went to work in the "oil patch" in the Texas panhandle country. They separated some years later, and Arleta returned to the Pawnee area (actually she lived and taught in Perry, Oklahoma – about 30 miles west of Pawnee,) where she taught school and finished raising her children. If Arleta were still alive, she would be in her nineties and likely still quiet and somewhat shy and reserved. I did not ever get to know her very well, primarily because of the considerable age difference, but also because of my living in greatly different parts of the country for about twenty-five years. Quilladean's first marriage was to Vernon who was an auto body mechanic and painter. They had three children together and Vernon died too early in life. Quilla's second marriage took her to Montana where she lived until just recently. Following her husband's (Chummy) death, she moved to the Texas panhandle near other family and where she dotes over her two rambunctious and small-but-loud dogs. In addition to her dogs is a rather large gathering of nieces and nephews and various grand and great-grandchildren. Judging from her "wall of books" Quilla spends a large amount of time enjoying good stories.

At this writing, Quilla is eighty-eight. That means she's still ten years older than I am. So, I guess I'll probably never catch up!

AUNT ALMA

Following Uncle Charlie's death in 1973, Aunt Alma sold their property in Pawnee and bought a house in Perry, about thirty miles west, where she lived until her death in 1989. Bonnie and I had many good visits with her, particularly after Bonnie's mother came to live with us. It didn't take very long for those two women to develop a great relationship. When they got together it was like watching two young schoolgirls making jokes about their boyfriends – their giggling was infectious. Bonnie and I believe this mutual relationship extended those two lives significantly. It may have even extended our lives as well!

THE SHAVE

I saw Uncle Charlie for the last time about fifteen years after leaving Pawnee. Working then as a pharmaceutical business market researcher, I had been assigned to a project that required me to visit surgeons and other operating room personnel, seeking input on surgical-scrub product requirements, needs, and desires. This visit took place in a hospital room in Tulsa, Oklahoma, in late 1973. I had heard that Uncle Charlie was in a Tulsa hospital; so, I scheduled some appointments in Tulsa, hoping to have opportunity to see him. It worked. Fortunately, his doctor was one that my cousin Norma worked for, and she helped me get permission to see Uncle Charlie. When I entered his room, I saw that he looked comfortable and that he was dozing. I sat and just watched for quite a while. Eventually he opened his eyes and noticed me. His eyes widened when he realized who he was looking at, and he produced a tired but sincere smile. We talked quietly for fifteen or twenty minutes, and during that time I noticed he had not been shaved for likely two or three days. I asked him if he would like a shave. With a weak and tired sounding voice he said that someone would probably take care of it later. And I said, "Uncle Charlie, I'd like to do it for you. Will you let me?" He looked at me and tears welled up in his eyes and he said, "Sure, I'd like that." He remained quiet as I lathered and shaved him, but every minute or so, a tear would trail down to his pillow. I never saw him again, but I will later. And I'm thankful for the opportunity I had to see and talk with him that one last time and to give him his last shave while he was alive. Uncle Charlie left us in August of 1973 at age seventy-two. Aunt Alma lived another sixteen years, her death being in September of 1989 at age eighty-four.

CHAPTER 5

X

…wickedness is an abomination to my lips.
Proverbs 8:7 (NKJV)

…but the name of the wicked will rot.
Proverbs 10:7 NKJV)

These scriptures above speak about everything X, I believe, was about and was indeed. For this writing and always in our minds, my sisters and I refer to our former step "father" only as X. Those who know something of our family at the time, will certainly remember who X was, so I see no reason to use his actual name. I choose to not give him, even in death, that dignity. To my brother, sisters, wife, and me, he represented the epitome of abomination and wickedness. Revealing his name would not, in any way, contribute to the story. He is deceased, as are my biological father, my mother and my brother. Those of us who were close or fairly close to these events include two cousins, my two sisters, my wife, and me. No family members of my mother's generation survive today.

MEETING X

On our return to Albuquerque from Pawnee, Oklahoma, where Mike and I had lived our adventures and good times with Aunt Alma and Uncle Charlie, and sister Mary had lived comfortably with our grandparents Plunkett, we met X for the first time. Mike, Mary and I, of course, did not know that we would be living and working on a sawmill location up in the mountains about 140 miles north and a bit west in a little more than a year. But early on, life with Mom, sis and X seemed quite good for brother Mike and me. We had fun riding horses, hunting gophers and rabbits, fishing for frogs and other things and swimming in the irrigation ditches with the water snakes and other water-liking creatures. X was well on his way into the building of a nice but not extravagant house, in what had been an asparagus field, a couple of miles west of the Rio Grande River and a little north of Route 66. The house, while mostly complete, still had considerable work to be done. Therefore, we lived in and around the construction, with the main living, eating, and kitchen areas being essentially finished. I believe we were on a small acreage, about 5 acres or so, that included a corral in the back part of the property, close to the irrigation ditch.

In the corral under a huge cottonwood tree we kept three riding horses, but we had no saddles for everyday use. The one saddle we did have was one X built and was virtually a piece of art with delicate tooling and lots of nickel-plated metal trim and which was intended for "show use" only. We believe X had learned leather working (boots, shoes, saddles, belts, etc.) in prison. Mike and I quickly became knowledgeable about our neighbors, most of whom had horses or access to horses. In retrospect, I believe it was in that time of our lives that Mike and I bonded very nicely and became good friends, the words "friend" and "brother" essentially becoming interchangeable, at least for a while. Our property was situated on the western most edge of Albuquerque and surrounded by other properties of similar size and purpose. All the "streets" had been built across asparagus fields and none was paved. So, lots of dust too!

MRS. PYLE'S HORSE

Our neighbor to the south, Mrs. Pyle, was, I believe, a nurse. (Note: Sometimes, when I mention Mrs. Pyle, people ask if she was related to Ernie Pyle, the WWII news correspondent, who was an Albuquerque resident. My answer has always been: I don't know, but I think not.) Her horse, she said, stood more than sixteen hands high. That's one or two hands (or four to eight inches) higher than any of the other riding horses we had. So, for us two young, short guys just to find someplace where we could manage to get atop the horse was often an issue. For those who are unfamiliar with measuring a horse's height, the correct terminology is "hands" in height. Height of a horse is measured from the forward hooves at ground level up to the top of the base of the neck (withers) – not to the top of the head. A "hand" is the unit of measure and a hand is equal to four (4) inches. Therefore, a "fifteen hand" measurement equals sixty (60) inches or five feet. Fifteen hands and two fingers equal 62 inches, etc. etc.

On one of our rides when we were crossing an irrigation ditch with water about four feet deep, the horse (whose name I do not remember) decided to lay down. This was a summer day in Albuquerque, so the weather was quite warm but the water, having come directly from the Rio Grande river, was quite cool. We had traveled a mile or so of graveled roadway upon reaching the irrigation canal. Our usual procedure at a canal, was to ride directly into the water (rather than staying on the road and using the bridge – because some horses are frightened by bridges) expecting to be on the other side in a minute or two. So, the horse deciding to lay down in the water, came as a complete surprise. And who was I to argue with a sixteen-hand horse? With only the horse's head and part of his neck above water, staying mounted was not an option.

Our trip back to Mrs. Pyle's property was uneventful, and it was, I believe, a nice walk. Neither of us could manage to mount the horse. Even if one of us did get mounted – with some help - how would the other get mounted? Thankfully, our clothes were mostly dry by the time we arrived at Mrs. Pyle's corral and shed. But our feet were complaining about the torture from walking on that gravel road because, as was our practice in the summer months, we were barefoot.

A FRIGHTENING CAMPSITE

The volcanic remains, west-northwest of downtown Albuquerque, are obvious and notable landmark formations that make it easy to establish almost exactly where you are with respect to the city of Albuquerque. They can be seen from almost anywhere in the city. Consequently, when we two horseback-riding brothers were headed westerly on horseback (which was our usual direction), we took our bearings on those volcanic formations. In this instance, we knew almost exactly where we wanted to be. Getting lost was almost impossible.

As was our usual pattern, we traveled about five or six miles west-northwest from what is now near or around NW 47th and Central Avenue on the west side of the Rio Grande. Petroglyph National Monument, established in 1990, lies generally west of Albuquerque and, consequently, west of the Rio Grande. In the 1940s that area was just another place to ride horses or camp. I believe we were often in those grounds on most of our westerly excursions. Also, I am sure, in those days, we were totally unaware of anything called "petroglyph." The Petroglyphs are certainly and obviously distinctive sights, but they seemed to not have made any sort of impression on Mike or me (or other folks of the time) who traveled into those areas on horseback. I have only vague recollection of what appeared, to me, to be graffiti. (Of course, I did not even know the word "graffiti" then either!)

My "Fire Pit Finding" section of this chapter contains several paragraphs that tell a story which may possibly have some relationship to these comments about petroglyphs. For perspective, let me explain that in 1949 and early 1950 the area in which we lived and had our horses, I believe, was only about a mile or two west of the Rio Grande River and less than a mile north of Central Avenue. Unser Boulevard at Central Avenue (today) is where one can turn north for a mile or two and access the Petroglyph monument grounds. In the late 1940s about all one could see and experience anywhere west and either north or south of that location was sand and sage brush along with horned toads, sheep droppings, the volcanos - and rattlesnakes. Unser Boulevard, in its present form, did not exist then, although I suppose some north-south roads across Route 66 had been cut by then.

In good weather we sometimes would make some sandwiches and gather up a few cans of pork 'n beans, and some ropes and tent materials and go out on horseback toward the volcanos into the sagebrush, gramma grass, and cactus. Sometimes for two or three nights. The major requirement was that Mom know when and where we were going and for how long. It was on one of our planned "overnighters" (this is the story I alerted you to two or three paragraphs back.) that Mike and I experienced a profound scare. We were so scared that we packed up our camping gear that we had unloaded, but not yet set up entirely, and "high tailed it" (to quote a Western phrase often used in the old Western movies and television shows) home.

Our fright was so profound that we ran (an easy lope, but faster than walking) the horses in the darkening evening. So, we were, in fact, "high tailing" it, which is something we ordinarily would not have done simply because of limited vision. But we were blessed with a bright moon that evening so, I guess, we felt comfortable moving at a faster than walk pace, and the horses were willing. The cause of this fright came about when we were digging our firepit. We wanted a fire to warm our cans of pork & beans while we finished the pup tent and made our bedrolls ready. By the way, the expression "high tailing" comes from the fact that a running horse or deer, lifts its tail, thus: it is "high tailing."

FIRE PIT FINDING

As a matter of practice when we camped out in the sagebrush and gramma grass areas we dug our fire pit at least a foot deep, after clearing away the brush and grasses, to reduce chances of starting a fire in the desert. Those were our instructions. We had a big bright moon early in the evening as our sunlight began to fade. As we dug we struck a hard surface that was, in that evening light, a pale gray color. As we dug deeper, thinking we had found a very nice large rock we could take home to Mom, we discovered this "rock" to have cracks and holes and other irregular features and shapes. Digging a bit deeper, we perceived a more definite shape or form and some features that looked like teeth. We had actually touched this thing with our bare hands too!

We didn't know for certain, (and I still don't know) but our decision was that we'd found a human skull. I was just thinking while writing this about how nice it might have been if Mike and I would have had the technology and the foresight to do a "selfie" that night. It would have been one that would have made noise on the "social media," I think. Provided, of course, that we would have had the required presence of mind to stop and pose and smile and get the angles right and be sure the "object" was well presented.

It took us, I believe, a nanosecond to decide we were going home, even with darkness coming on. On arriving home, it was obvious to Mom and X that we were scared. Almost immediately Mom phoned the county sheriff's office to report this finding. She was told they would see us 'first thing in the morning' and that we were to be prepared to take them out to the site. Sleep was certainly difficult to achieve that night. It was about daybreak when the sheriff and two deputies arrived in two pickups, each pulling a horse trailer. They had six saddled horses with them.

With Mike in the lead and me talking with one of the sheriff's deputies, we headed toward the site of our discovery. We knew exactly where to go! But before we had departed, Mike and I asked to have the saddles removed from the horses we were to ride. We were unaccustomed to saddles and couldn't reach the stirrups anyway.

About a week later we received a visitor from the sheriff's office who informed us that our "object" had been turned over to "proper authorities" for disposition. We never heard anything else about it. While Mike and I were not particularly anxious to see what was removed from our fire pit, the fact is that we didn't. The Sheriff's deputies had sort of screened us off during the digging and placed the "object" in a canvas bag, never giving us an opportunity to look at it, not that I'm very sure we even wanted to see it. But I am happy to say the event did not deter our desires to camp in those sand and sagebrush lands to the northwest. I think I'm also happy to say that the event with pictures did not make the local news.

Whether the area Mike and I were in that evening is/was in fact an ancient burial grounds, I do not know. The police said they would "advise" us of any conflicts regarding this event. We never heard from anyone about it. And some seventy years later, we still haven't. And I haven't changed my name yet either! I think, at this point, Mike and I (if he were still with us) would agree that the "object" was probably nothing more than a piece of lava or rock that over the years and decades (if not centuries) had been covered over with sand, perhaps several times. But whatever it was, Mike and I were the cause of a bit of excitement. And, having mentioned petroglyph items earlier, I do not recall ever seeing any of them in our travels in that area, although it is entirely possible we did and just didn't know what they were or even realize they had been created by humans eons ago! It is entirely possible we linked anything we may have seen to simple graffiti and never gave it a second thought. However, it's also doubtful that we even knew the word "graffiti" and therefore its implications. Sometimes ignorance is bliss. Really!

BARBED WIRE AND SCARS

Barbed wire fences were common everywhere around us. Neighbors had large gardens that needed protection from horses who had cravings for fresh vegetables. They like lettuce and carrots in particular! Other neighbors had mares that seemed to always be "in heat" thereby causing the neighboring males of the equine species, who were capable of creating offspring, considerable anxiety. It was not uncommon for those "males of the species" to harm themselves when they tried to access the mares by attempting to go over or through some of those barbed-wire fences. We had only one male and he was older and had been neutered. So, he didn't care one way or the other! However, Mike and I were exposed on one occasion to a horse that had gotten himself hung up on top of a steel fence post. He had to be put down. Sad, very sad.

Our large corral being back by the irrigation canal, made it necessary to cross an acre or two of asparagus and climb or go through a fence or two to get the horses. We rarely used the gates when it was just Mike and me walking out toward the corral because opening and closing them just took too much time. When Mrs. Pyle wanted us to ride her roan horse, for the exercise, our main problem was getting mounted. We always rode bareback because, as mentioned elsewhere, we didn't have a saddle and getting a horse saddled would likely have been too great a problem for two little guys anyway. Therefore, our first job was to get the horse someplace where one of us could mount it. One day, when it was my turn to ride the roan, I climbed atop one of the fence posts as Mike brought the horse to me. For us two small guys, it was easy to perch right on top of one of the wood fence posts to mount any of the horses. But we for sure needed to be up high to mount that sixteen-hand horse. I wasn't quite ready to launch myself across about two feet of space to the horse when it moved sideways toward me. In my surprise I lost footing and balance only to get myself hung up on the top row of barbed wire. Those scars, too, are still visible on my upper chest, which added three more scars to accompany those from the chain-link fence in Pawnee some months earlier. I'm not sure, but it seems possible I simply crawled back on the fence post, and we went riding anyway. Maybe not. I might run out of scar stories in this writing, but I doubt it.

KILLING A HOG

My belief is that the building of the house on Lake Road, on ground that had once been part of a frequently cultivated field, was never entirely completed. It seems we had sawhorses, tools, and lumber always laying around someplace, waiting for the next "phase." But very clear in my mind are images of the horse corral in the "back" part of the acreage we were on. Barbed wire fences established our property lines and separated rows of asparagus plantings from grazing areas. The fences also separated the crop fields from the banks of an irrigation canal across the back side of the property. We had no trees, no lawn, no hard surface driveway or even an asphalt street. It was all sand and dirt which contributed to clouds of dust when the winds were up. The house itself was essentially built. We were living in it. The living room, dining area, kitchen and bathroom were complete. I distinctly recall the walls of the living room being finished in varnished tongue and groove knotty-pine planks. Very attractive! Three of the four bedrooms were still unfinished. One of those rooms was being used for food storage and included a large almost room sized freezer: sort of a newfangled contraption in those days.

The butchering event began with the delivery of a large hog which was placed inside the horse corral. A block and tackle device had been hung in the cottonwood tree that shaded the corral. Then came the job of killing and butchering the hog. X seemed to be a man of many skills and talents that included enough knowledge of butchering to tackle that job. His first mistake, however, was his attempt to kill the hog with a .22 caliber semiautomatic rifle. The rifle was loaded with hollow point rounds. Regardless, however, with the muzzle of the rifle pressed against the skull of the hog and the firing of several rounds into its head, the hog refused to die. In fact, it broke through the corral fence and ran into the asparagus field where X ran after it, jumped on its back, and finally cut its throat.

The hog eventually bled out, but not before spreading a lot of blood around the asparagus field. But then came the problem of getting this very large hog (probably more than 200 pounds) suspended from the block and tackle for butchering. I'm sure night came on and the moon was up and bright and then the sun was rising before we finished getting all that meat into the freezer. I'm also sure Mom was quite pleased that none of us, Mike, me or X, had gotten even a speck of dirt or blood on our clothes. Well, maybe that was in my dream that next night, which came very early!

DISCIPLINE ISSUES

A bit more than a year following our return from living with Aunt Alma and Uncle Charlie, things seemed at peace. Having nearly completed fourth grade for me and third grade for Mike and having become accustomed to good meals and comfortable beds in the new house, life was easy, pleasant and seemingly un- complicated. Mike and I had a few new friends and Mary seemed to be forming into a real person, meaning we could kid and clown around with her without her becoming upset or irritated. I believe Mike and I, along with Sis, were adjusting to a degree to our new environment, i.e., someone new in the house. Meaning, of course, X. Maybe it was related to the "Alpha Male" establishment of dominance in the household, or maybe it was more about a misguided idea on how a person continues the rearing of the children of another man. Or, perhaps the behavior was learned from his own childhood. Whatever the background, I question whether Mom, before their agreement to marry, had ever discussed with X any of his ideas or beliefs concerning rearing children. Whatever the background and circumstance and level(s) of agreement on child rearing and other family "issues" Mom and X may have established, it seems some of them began to fall apart near the end of their second year of marriage.

FEAR FACTOR

Close to the end of the school year of my fourth grade and before the completion of the house on Lake Road came a time when I had been left "in charge" of Mike and Mary Sue while Mom and X "went out for dinner." When they arrived home a couple hours later, they found the three of us all involved in jumping on and off furniture, yelling, laughing, and enjoying ourselves to the nth degree. That was the eve of the beginning of understanding the pain and fright of being whipped with a leather belt. Added to the trauma of this event was the frightening yelling, cursing, and grabbing and holding each of us down with one hand and striking with the belt using the other hand.

I do not know if blood was drawn, but I do know about deep purple and blue and black bruises each of us came away with. Frightening indeed! In retrospect the demeanor of X was evidence of his being "out of control." I'm not sure if Mom tried to stop him, but if she did try, she failed. Also, if she did try, it seems possible and probable she was hit as well. The principal thing here is that this event established a "fear factor" in the minds of Mike, Sis, and me. All X had to do whenever an event or circumstance involved some actual or perceived bad behavior on our part, was for him to touch the buckle on the belt around his waist. That was enough to persuade any one or all of us to stop whatever we were doing.

WE NEVER CALLED HIM "DAD"

It was probably some subconscious perception that Mike, Sis, and I shared that resulted in our never referring to X as "Dad" or "Father." Nor did we use his given name. In those years it seems most families observed the custom of a child not addressing either of his parents by a given name, but instead tending to use a title like "mom" or "father." Mike and I, however, for whatever reason, would only use a form of the words "he" or "you." I am unaware of that choice being a conscious decision initially. It is possible, if not probable, that we used "Yes sir" and "No sir" when conversing directly with him. In retrospect it seems Mike and I had both reached a level of discomfort with him that resulted in our never considering the use of a name or title other than "sir." To attempt citing a specific rationale or reason for omission of name or title on the parts of Mike or me early in our relationship would be fruitless. Eventually, however, a certain level of contempt for him came into existence due to the kind of discipline he exercised following actual or perceived misbehavior.

OUR SONS CALLED ME "DAD"

During the writing of this project, thus far, my thoughts have seemed often to drift toward moments in the past shared with my own two sons,

Michael and Robert. Admittedly, I missed a good portion of time spent with them in both military and then my "corporate world" days when my work would frequently take me out of town, sometimes for several days (and in the case of military needs, weeks or months) in a row. My longest time away during my Navy years was a fourteen month stretch in Viet Nam in 1966 and '67 assigned to a U.S. Marine Corps unit – "HooRah!". Also, in 1961 I was aboard a U.S. Navy ship during a seven month long "WESTPAC" (Western Pacific) cruise. (See Chapter 19) But I do recall with pleasure the many times we three would spend time in the backyard roughhousing or playing ball or just goofing off. We went on trips together and spent time working on homework or doing some chore around the house. I regret those times I had to be away on business and the military assignments overseas.

As our sons matured and they began having "girl troubles," it pleased me when one or the other asked my "advice" on "certain" things. However, I also sometimes felt at a loss because of the lack of such advice in my own teenage years. But at another level, this was likely a blessing in disguise because occasionally certain research was necessary for us "uninformed" parents to respond appropriately to the needs of our children. Bonnie was much better at that; probably because she is much less impatient than I am. However, it seems fair to conclude that I enjoyed some amount of success in that area because my sons always called me "Dad." Our son, Robert, still does! Our son Michael would if he were still here.

WHAT WE DID NOT LEARN

The following commentary concerns some thoughts about male youth growing up without a true father figure. I'm not venturing into social commentary concerning "proper" parenting and related issues. Instead, I wish to relate some of my impressions about how Mike and I, as young boys, were never exposed (except for our one-year-plus of living with Uncle Charlie and Aunt Alma) to adequate and proper male supervision, mentoring, and leadership as we entered our teen age years and beyond.

In many ways Mike and I supported and mentored each other. I think this happened because a "father figure" was never presented in any believable or realistic way to us through our step "father." Support of and interest in things Mike and I wanted and enjoyed and became involved in after our relocation to Pawnee were never underwritten nor encouraged by X.

In fact, many were ridiculed and scoffed at and labeled as "unmanly" or "sissy." Mike wanted to pursue study of mechanical engineering and music. My interests leaned toward chemistry and math, and writing. We each eventually went into, in some ways, our desired fields of interest but without the benefit of higher education at the collegiate level. I am not saying that everybody should necessarily seek higher education. Some do not want to. Some do not need to. Some just simply could not qualify. But everybody who wants to should at least have the opportunity to try. Pursuing higher education, it seems to me, should be the result of interest, ability, and means. This includes and even requires, in my judgement, familial support and encouragement, neither of which Mike nor I ever received during our high school years. Both of us, however, took advantage of learning opportunities during our military years. Mike received education in machining, machinery, and design. My higher learning was in health care and pharmacy related sciences and study. And both of us enjoyed the benefits of those educational endeavors for the rest of our lives.

———————— ✳ ————————

CHAPTER 6

A Three-Wheel Motorcycle and a Broken Leg

Upon our return from Pawnee, Oklahoma, to Albuquerque we learned of our stepfather and got reacquainted with Mom and Mary Sue. First, we lived in a garage apartment attached to or near the house of Uncle Coy and Aunt Neva. By our return to Albuquerque, X had already started construction on the new house about a mile or so west of the Rio Grande and a little north of Highway 66 on what was called, I believe, Lake Road, discussed in limited detail in Chapter 5.

If you are looking at a local Albuquerque map, you'll notice no lakes exist in that area. It seems possible, however, that lakes once did, eons ago, hence its proximity to the Rio Grande River. Thus, the possibility of lake beds still in evidence. Maybe even lakes of lava at some point? But, suffice to say, lakes of water, if any, had been long gone by 1948. The magnificent Rio Grande, beginning in south central Colorado, flows over a thousand miles to Brownsville, Texas, on the Gulf Coast. On its way it creates part of the border between the USA and Mexico from El Paso to Brownsville. The river essentially separates all of New Mexico and Albuquerque, east from west. Sometime in the fourth grade early in 1949, I suffered a compound fracture of both bones of my lower left leg. This happened while riding on top of the back of a three-wheel motorcycle that X was driving. We were on a bumpy sand and gravel road across what had been one of those asparagus fields when I got bounced off and run over. After more than seventy years the large "S" scar on that leg is still quite visible being about eight or nine inches long. (So, here's yet another scar story!) Two screws were used to hold the tibia together and, I believe one screw was used in the fibula. Through the years I have sometimes thought about whether the scar would have been longer if I had grown taller. I only made it to about five and one-half feet. I'll wager that if I had made six feet, the scar would be a foot long. Maybe? Maybe not.

During my recovery, I got along fine, mostly. Sometimes, however, when other kids would mock or tease me, my hot side would light up, and then I'd be in trouble with the teacher. A crutch makes a good weapon, I discovered. Another discovery a bit later was that I could outrun some of the kids, even with my crutches. Having three points on the ground and full use of both arms, was an advantage! One of the unhappy things that happened was when red ants invaded and took up residence inside my cast, which went from my toes to my upper thigh. I learned to have a straightened-out clothes hanger to help deal with that sort of problem. Red ants in Albuquerque are plentiful and they grow big! Perhaps my short stature was really an advantage by limiting space for more ants!

One of the great mysteries I experienced during the time of healing was my being taken to the home of one of the employees of the Atomic Energy facility in Los Alamos, north and west of Santa Fe. Two specific things I remember from that visit were: first, the interest in photography of the homeowner where I stayed, and secondly, the absolute order and cleanliness of the small city in the mountains. Everything seemed to sparkle. And the city swimming pool was about the brightest thing I guess I had ever seen. Of course, Mike and I had been accustomed to muddy irrigation ditches!

Even the city public transportation sparkled. The "sparkle" of Los Alamos probably was because of all the federal money coming into that town in support of the Atomic Energy Commission and Dr. Albert Einstein. This remote town, by the way, has the nickname of "Lost Almost", because it is! Why I was placed with this family, which included a daughter about my age, I never knew. And I have no recollection of where Mike and Sis were during that time. I remember being impressed with the photographs the "man of the house" had shot, printed, and framed. That work undoubtedly influenced my own interest in photography. The big question, however, was about the exact relationship that, somehow, included X. I have no recollection of any kind of thought or discussion about this visit to Dr. Einstein's town and the family I stayed with for those few weeks and whose names I cannot recall.

The timing here is a little fuzzy, but I believe it was sometime later in the house-building time that Mike and I were taken on a long motorcycle ride up into the northwest mountains of New Mexico west of the Continental Divide. We stayed overnight in an old weather-beaten cabin where we had bacon and eggs with water for supper, and eggs and bacon with coffee for breakfast before returning to Albuquerque. Those meals were prepared on the top of a Pot-belly wood burning stove. It did not occur to me until this writing, but that trip may have been our first visit to the sawmill area. I do recall that the trip took most of a full day, one way, which included at least four hours of dirt roads until we reached the cabin. That then, seems consistent with the same 130 or 140-mile trip of today, with at least 40 miles of it on dirt roads if one travels via Lindrith and Ojito instead of going north on Highway 537 - which did not exist until sometime near 1960.

Old highway 44 that took the traveler northwest from Bernalillo to Bloomfield and on to Aztec, NM, is today numbered 550. Maps of the

69

time (see the Map Pages) show that the only paved roads in the Jicarilla Apache Indian Reservation were portions of Highway 44 (now 550) in the south and Highway 17 (now 64) in the north. But what a trip on that three-wheeled motorcycle! Mike and I both contracted TB on that very long trip! (In this case TB stands for Tired Behinds.)

REAL HALF DOLLARS

In late 1949 construction of the house on Lake Road had been completed to a point where we could live in it with relative comfort. Three horses were in the corral and neighborhood garden plots were harvested and plowed and waiting for Springtime. Fences and corral and gates were repaired. Mike and I had made a couple of friends with whom we explored our new neighborhood. And we still had some frozen hog meat left. We had visits from our nearby cousins and aunts and uncles and life seemed good, mostly. Mike, Mary and I were enrolled into the Old Armijo Schools. Mary started first grade that year, Mike went to third grade and I to fourth grade. It was close to or right after the end of this school year when we loaded up and headed for The Sawmill.

One of my fourth grade pals was also a neighbor. His name was Wayne and by anybody's book, he was a "spoiled-rotten kid." His father was a columnist, I believe, for the Albuquerque newspaper. Wayne always had money it seemed (even in 4th grade) and new, fresh, clean clothes and "slicked back" hair every day. He delighted in showing off his silver half dollars. His favorite way of demonstrating his possession of that cash was to throw it away. Yep, he really did! He would bring several of those silver half dollars (pure silver in those years) to school, and during recess go to the playgrounds and throw them just to watch the rest of us dig in the sand to find them. The thing of it was that the school yards of the Old Armijo School were almost totally sand. No grass and very few concrete areas existed that I can remember. I had limited opportunity to chase after the money because a large part of that time was when I was on crutches with the broken leg. Later I think I was able to snag a half dollar or so, but I'm not actually sure of that. I just wonder how many were never found because the sand was very fine and more than several inches deep. Wayne threw them as hard as he could and, being flat, they sailed pretty good, so he got some distance and they would just "slice" into the loose New Mexico sand. Sometimes, Wayne could even "skip" them as one can skip flat stones over water. If I could just remember the location of the school and if it isn't now covered by more buildings or parking lots or streets and sidewalks, I could use my metal detector and go find some of those half dollars that were lost in the sand. Certainly, those half dollars are worth much more than fifty cents apiece today!

CHAPTER 7

The Fire and the Move

I cannot view a truckload of raw lumber or a sawmill
without thinking about the sawmill.

…the tongue is a little member and boasts great things.
See how great a forest a little fire kindles. And the tongue is a fire,
a world of iniquity. The tongue is so set among our members that it
defiles the whole body and sets on fire the course of nature;
and it is set on fire by hell.
James 3:5-6 (NKJV)

Like the tongue, fire can be either good or bad. It is when the
tongue and brain, along with fire, combine for reasons that are
not good when bad things can happen to good people. This seems to have
been the case for my biological family and me in early May of 1950.

Memory is not clear about the exact date in 1950, but it was close to
May 3rd, the day of birth of my younger sister, Donna. I was soon to be
eleven. Mary, the older of my two sisters, had just turned seven a month
earlier; and my brother Mike was eighteen months my junior and we were

still good friends, mostly. We lived in our near-new, yet still unfinished, house on the west side of Albuquerque, not far from the Rio Grande River and about half a mile north of Highway 66. Mom was in the hospital, birthing (or just following birthing) baby sister Donna. Mike, Mary and I had been taken to a movie at the Sandia Theater on Central Avenue. It was a "cops and robbers" story I believe, or maybe a Lash LaRue western. When we heard the sirens, I thought it was part of the movie. But it wasn't. Emergency vehicles were headed to our house. So, disregard the idea of a Lash Larue Western! The house didn't burn to the ground, but we couldn't live in it.

We kids were "farmed out" to willing neighbors who provided sleeping and bathing facilities and some of our meals. I cannot recall whether we finished out the school year, but my belief is that we did not. On the second and third days following the fire we were a little bit reorganized and beginning to focus on what to do about clothes and other needs. It was on the third day following the fire, that Mom got Mike, Mary, and me together and explained to us the need to find clothing. Each of us had been placed with a willing family for a place to sleep and eat but Mom opined that they should not be asked to provide clothing also.

At the time, we did not realize how badly we were going to need those clothes – especially the heavy coats and jackets and gloves. Albuquerque, at about five thousand feet elevation, means daytime temperatures can be chilly and nighttime temperatures will cool significantly, even in May and early June. Our neighborhood was not what you would call "affluent," so the handout clothing we were able to get was not always the best, but it was at least clean and wearable. Sometimes, to have all skin covered on our legs and be a little more presentable, meant wearing more than one pair of jeans at a time. Contrast that to today's fashion statements that seem to demand holes, rips and tears in jeans. But fashion or not, our overriding concern was to keep our legs warm. Mary recalls wanting to search in the burned house for her dolls – but no one was being allowed to enter. So, in our search for clothes, we also asked about dolls for Mary. That made her happy and better to live with! By the way, having said what I just said, I have a strong inclination to comment unfavorably about today's "fashion" statements and ideas regarding ruined jeans! I'll see if I can resist the urge! Well, maybe later I'll comment – I need to stay with my current train of thought for now.

The actual date of our move to the sawmill is unknown to me, but it was not long after the fire. Our arrival on the sawmill site, as mentioned elsewhere, was possibly late in May but more likely early-to-mid June 1950. Recollection of discussion about timing or time of year is sparse at best. However, the application of logic seems to support the idea that we had several months of good weather that allowed us to accomplish as much as we did in terms of harvesting trees and making lumber before the higher altitude freezing temperatures and snowfall arrived at the sawmill.

THE ODOR OF CATASTROPHE

Any way you slice it, a house fire is a catastrophe. Even though no one died or was even injured (physically) in this fire, the consequences, nonetheless, were staggering. For me, it was the smell. Once you have experienced the odor of the remains of a house fire, you'll not forget that odor, for it is the compilation of many different odors at once. It is not just the odor of a burned package of meat nor that of burned knotty-pine wood paneling. It's not just the odor of scorched shoe leather or melted rubber boots or burnt underwear. It's not just the odor of melted plastic handles of pots and pans or of a plastic or rubber play-doll. It's not just the odor of scorched furniture stuffing or heat-damaged painted or varnished wood parts, or a completely burned loaf of bread. And it is not just the odor of water-soaked and burnt blankets and sheets and pillows and mattresses. It is the odor of destruction, of things lost forever, of certain kinds of memories and disappointment, and of the difficult road to recovery. And how does one describe the odor of the loss of security and lifestyle? Finally, how does one adequately and accurately describe the horrible odor of a probable, intentionally set house fire?

I believe Mike and I, at ages nine and near eleven, did not fully comprehend the damage done, primarily because we actually saw very little of it. No one was allowed inside the burned structure for safety reasons, especially youngsters like Mike, Mary, and me. What we did know was that we could recover absolutely nothing from inside the house because it was deemed unsafe to go inside. Add to that the fact that within a very few days or weeks, we were on the road to the sawmill. But in the meantime, it was also the chore of assimilating and understanding the extent and meaning of this tremendous loss. This subsequent total "change of scenery" represented a complete change of almost everything else we had been doing or thinking of doing. Our focus had changed from finding something for lunch or supper to finding a new way to live. It went from learning something new at school to learning how to harvest a sixty or seventy-foot-tall pine tree. In a word, our situation was catastrophic. It stunk! It was, without question, the odor of catastrophe.

Part II
Work in the Wilderness

CHAPTER 8

Where Are We?

I sought the Lord, and He heard me, and delivered me from all my fears.
Psalm 34:4 (NKJV)

If memory serves correctly, we three kids and Baby DJ (about five weeks old) rode with mom in the car following X in the truck as we moved from Albuquerque to the sawmill most likely sometime in late May or early-to-mid June of 1950. The highway travel was probably okay. But some forty or fifty miles of rough and bumpy dirt roads through pine and scrub-oak forests, sage brush and sand, and the unfamiliar country took its toll. Even worse, if it was not riding over the bad roads that might have put us into shock, the site of the sawmill area certainly could have.

We didn't know about prayer then, but if we had, I'm sure we would have been on our knees in a flash. The question "Where are we?" was soon replaced by "Why are we here?" and later it became "How long will we be here?" The "fear factor" persisted for quite a while but finally receded, at least to some degree. How much security could we have felt and believed in if we had known God then?

At this writing, a little over sixty-eight years have come and gone since the day of the house fire. But I still retain very clear memories of many of the things that happened to my brother, my sisters, my mother, and me during those next fifteen or sixteen months. At the same time, certainly my brain has locked out or forgotten much of what happened. This writing, then, concerns itself with those memories that my sisters and I do have, and can articulate, of living and working and surviving in the strange and seemingly threatening mountains at the sawmill. I remember arriving for the first time on the sawmill grounds. I remember because, as an eleven-year-old (on May 28, 1950), the unfamiliar, empty and stark atmosphere was silent and frightening.

Curiosity, being one of my traits, likely prompted me to ask something like: "Where are we?" Standing beside the truck and looking at four little cabins (more properly called "shacks") on a low hill sloping toward the canyon just east of us, I remember feeling confused and maybe even frightened. The shacks, we quickly learned, were our new living quarters and a kitchen. To my right, as I looked down the hill, I saw several large logs laying in a pile and some strange looking equipment built right up to the edge of the cliff. That strange looking equipment didn't look quite so strange a couple of weeks later, for it was the sawmill apparatus.

Even though we had traveled a total of about 140 miles from Albuquerque in the old green International flat-bed truck and the car, we had been "on the road" for most of the day. The last 70 or so miles of paved highway from Bernalillo was a steady climb of about 2500 feet of altitude after crossing the Rio Grande River and accessing Highway 44 toward Cuba. About fifteen miles northwest of Cuba on Highway 44 would have been where we turned directly north and drove dirt roads another 40 or so miles to the sawmill. Those roads took us through the trees and hills and canyons on the way to the sawmill site.

The sawmill area was just beyond the rise (Photo April 2018)

One question must have been: What happened to cause us to be here in this place up in the mountains? The answer came much later - even long after we left the mountains and were in Oklahoma. The answer came by way of two of my uncles who had been living and working in Albuquerque in 1950. They knew.

I knew, even at 10 years of age, that X was a serious and aggressive player of table games, but card games generally and poker specifically. And every appearance (I figured out much later from overheard talk between my uncles Coy and Ward.) was that we had arrived at this remote sawmill location in the mountains, not because of happenstance or luck (good or bad), but by design. I believe the sawmill had been won in a poker game! And the poker game must have been prior to the destruction by fire of our newly built (but incomplete) house on Lake Road in Albuquerque, New Mexico. Suppose the poker game theory is true. It follows then, that to take advantage of the win, would require converting either the property you already had or the one you won in the poker game, into cash. We will almost certainly never know for sure what the truth really was about motive, but what we do know is that the decisions that were made, impacted in serious and negative ways, our entire family. And the impact was felt by most of the extended family as well. Think mogul. And, quite frankly, this impact of profound proportions remained significant for decades. Indeed, just the writing of this very story represents IMPACT. I will have more discussion on the idea of the poker game win of the sawmill in Chapter 13, "Leaving and Arriving," where I will link that theory to other things that "happened" in Pawnee.

Logic suggests that we entered the sawmill site sometime between the last week of May, and the middle of June following the May 3rd house fire. Therefore, it was very close to, if not on, my eleventh birthday on May 28. Mike would be ten in November and Mary would have just turned seven about six weeks prior. As the old truck labored up that last hill and we entered the clearing, we could see evidence of past habitation. We saw what appeared to be recent tire tracks in the dirt, ashes from a scrap heap burn perhaps a week or so old, and cigarette butts not yet deteriorated. This area of perhaps eight or ten acres, was mostly void of trees and extended out to the edge of the canyon to the east.

A large water tank mounted on a trailer sat to the west of the shacks higher up the hill. We found inside one of the shacks many tools including a couple of "two-man" crosscut saws, double-bit axes, single-bit axes, sledgehammers, chains, harness, and several other things, some totally unfamiliar. But they became familiar in short order! One of them, a tool for maneuvering the logs called a cant hook, became all too familiar. You'll find more "tool" discussion later.

To the east and a little north of the "living" area, the land showed a gradual downward slope toward the mill machinery which was positioned very close to the cliff edge. The sawdust chute extended over the canyon rim, and below can still be seen today mounds of sawdust and pieces of rotted scrap lumber. North of the machinery area was a good entrance to the canyon floor, a four or five-foot wide "path" down to the bottom. This pathway seems, in the satellite imagery, largely unchanged from the time we lived and worked at the sawmill.

View "up the hill" from the sawmill site at canyon edge. (Photo April 2018)

This wide pathway provided easy access for taking the horses to water and, of course, when we kids wanted to go to the canyon floor. At that time, this part of the canyon floor was almost barren of trees. Imagery today shows a thick growth of trees on the southwest side, probably due to the spring having been re-drilled to a fresh water supply. The canyon was named "Iron Spring" back then. And "back then" the spring water was extremely hard, thus, "Iron" Spring. The taste of iron was quite discernable. The canyon, I'm guessing, is about eighty to one hundred feet deep at this point. A fence line is today almost directly in the center of the canyon floor, running north/south. It serves to mark the East boundary of the far West section of Carson National Forest. During our time on the Sawmill, no fence line marked the boundary between Carson National Forest and the Jicarilla Apache Indian Reservation. Further, I have not researched the timeline of the designation of boundaries for the various segments of Carson NF lands so it seems possible that those lands had not even been designated and/or identified in 1950.

Upon learning we kids would not be going to school, my guess is that by this time in our lives, we simply shrugged our shoulders and muttered something like, "Well, so what's new?" For it seemed that on a frequent basis, we were subjected to one kind or another of "changes in plans" or "differing circumstances" or any number of other situations concerning a full slate of crazy and outlandish things that were happening. I hasten to add, however, that I strongly suspect that Mike and I weren't particularly upset at not being "able" to get to school! Also, just for perspective, the closest schools were likely either in Dulce, about 30 miles north, or Cuba, about 40 miles southeast. Dulce, however, being in the reservation (clearly identified in maps of the time) would probably have been inaccessible to us since we have no American Indian heritage.

As a side note, during my years working in the pharmaceutical field and at one point residing in Delaware working in the headquarter facility, my Oklahoma roots earned me the title of "Oklahoma red-headed Indian." All in fun of course – and that was when I had an ample cropping of red hair! I doubt that initially any family or friends, except an aunt and uncle in Albuquerque, knew where we were. However, I did know that some familial postal correspondence occurred from time to time and that it had to be picked up in Ojito, some 24 or 25 miles of rutted and rough dirt roads to the east-southeast. (See the area maps at the front of this book.)

2018 VISITS TO THE SAWMILL SITE

For our visits to this area in early April 2018 we had immediate access to Road 314 through a cattle-guard gate at the extreme southeast corner of the westernmost section of Carson NF. The road was easy to follow, but we encountered a locked gate about four miles in that made it necessary for us to hike another approximately two miles toward the canyon area we needed to access. Bonnie and I are not as agile or strong or, perhaps, smart as we used to be. And this hike, at its relatively high altitude, is a bit of a challenge for people like us. Altitude sickness became an issue for Bonnie. So, next trip, we shall be better prepared. I am pleased, however, that we were able to get a few photographs (some of which are herein) of the area which gives the reader at least a good idea of the general landscape. Of course, none of the old machinery or structures are on the property and regrowth of trees and other foliage certainly changes the landscape. When one views satellite images of the area, all the gas well sites are easy to identify, and all those sites are visited regularly so the roads are easy to follow.

The challenge here is to stay on your bearing and not get turned around given all the gas well sites, many of which designate the end of that particular road. It's very easy to get "turned around" and therefore, lost. Also, almost any amount of significant rainfall makes those clay-based roads impassable. Should we attempt to make this trip again, which might very well happen, it will include checking with some of the people who work those gas wells about a better way to access Iron Spring canyon. However, my visit with a couple of those guys on this trip yielded no significant help. Maybe better luck next time! Just as a warning: If you should decide to attempt finding Iron Spring canyon (where the actual spring is) you must be very "direction" oriented, so use a compass!! Secondly, in the bottom of the canyon is a fence line that separates the reservation (Jicarilla Indian) from Carson NF and it runs north/south. So, if you decide to try climbing the fence to get to the spring, just be sure you're up to it. Also, word is that Black Bears are gaining in population in that area, so beware! Take a weapon. This applies, of course, whether you climb the fence or go through the gas well sites. Finally, I am no expert nor authority concerning rules and regulations for being on National Forest grounds, so just be sure you are up to speed on what is legal and what isn't! Check the web sites and/or make a phone call or two. Just be safe and be legal!

A WORD ROAD MAP TO THE SAWMILL SITE

ACCESS: Via Road 314 entering Carson NF extremely close to the southeast corner of the far western section of Carson. This entrance is within sight – almost - of Highway 537. Our understanding is that all entrances to Carson NF are open from late March to late October – but check first. Penetrate the fence at the cattle-guarded entrance – about a mile north (on the dirt road) of the Compressor Station facility just off Highway 537. You are now on Road 314. Follow Road 314 westerly (it winds around but generally runs west until you reach Cottonwood Canyon. I don't know the actual distance, but it will approximate two miles. Then turn right to enter a canyon, marked with a sign announcing, "Cottonwood Canyon." Your heading now is NNE and is a continuation of Road 314. It runs a relatively straight course and is blocked by a locked gate at a gas-well site in about two miles. Park the vehicle in a place out-of-the-way of potential gas-well trucks that might be visiting the well site. Then comes a hike of about two-and-a-half miles north by northeast and still on Road 314 to the farthest north well-head site. Then take a bearing of east north east toward the canyon. The distance here I estimate at another one-half mile, but you have no trail to follow. Therefore, take your bearing, ENE, select a visual target, and walk toward it. Keep selecting visual targets on the same bearing until you reach the canyon rim. Then follow the rim straight north, a very short distance, to a large clearing that should reveal a good sighting of the open canyon to your right (east). I used EARTH Maps Satellite 2018 to prepare for this exercise. That site allows printing of the images – which has been quite beneficial.

NOTE 1: The canyon below the sawmill site is very likely accessible from the east side of Iron Spring canyon. The last half mile (or so) today involves being on foot to enter the canyon from the east and climbing the fence on the floor of Iron Spring Canyon to get into the Carson National Forest. The west side of the canyon at that point appears (via satellite image) to be negotiable – as it was in 1950. Grid Coordinates are: 36, 33' 38" N, and 107, 11' 36" W.

NOTE 2: The U.S. Forest Service station servicing the westernmost section of Carson NF is at 1110 Rio Vista Lane, Unit #2, Bloomfield, NM 87413. Phone 505 632-2956 and Fax 505 632-3173. Website: www. fs.usda.gov/carson.

COMMERCIAL SAWMILL BLADE PORTION.

Blade diameter, approximately 44 inches

Saw Tooth length, approximately 3 inches, tip-to-tip.

CHAPTER 9

The Work

Man goes out to his work and to his labor until the evening.
Psalm 104:23 (NKJV)

Taken literally, the scripture above implies that "man" must work. It seems also to imply that work should be a daily experience, except (as noted elsewhere) to observe the sabbath. It also, for me, implies an "honest" day's work. In 1950 neither Mike nor I could be referred to as "men" even though we did men's work. Of course, that has happened throughout the world for centuries. And while we have "child labor laws" today, I believe they did not exist in the 1950s – at least not to any substantial extent. So, it was what it was. But to be clear, the "work" part was not nearly as rough as was the "treatment" part.

THE WORK PART

To an eleven-year-old kid a sixty or seventy-foot-tall pine tree with a two foot or more diameter trunk at the bottom looks mighty daunting. Add to that a double-bit ax with a three-foot-long handle and a two-man crosscut saw that is longer than he is tall. These are intimidating tools, especially when he has had no experience with them. Then comes the prospect of learning how and under what circumstances these tools are to be used. Finally, the realization emerges that these two tools are what he and his younger brother will use to bring down, remove limbs from, and cut into sections this huge tree whose top he can just barely see. The only trees that could be harvested were those marked by the Forest Service people, so we could not "practice" on some smaller ones first. It was under the watchful eye of X that Mike and I began learning how to use these tools. X's first admonition, to his credit, consisted of stern warnings about safety. (I guess I could express a certain kind of critique here, but I won't.) He did, however, make the point that our location, being far away from any sort of medical facility, demanded we observe all the rules of safe use of these tools.

The common work rules were about keeping sharp tools sharp and all tools clean, in good repair and lubricated as required. No dirt or mud on the handles, no rusty and nicked cutting edges, and handles properly fitted and secure. To X's credit, he was adamant about our following those work rules. He also made it clear that neither Mike nor I would be expected to handle a horse or horse team to move cut logs to the mill area. He would do that. Speaking of horses causes me to think back to our times in northwest Albuquerque where we rode horses almost daily. And we didn't just ride them casually. We went on camping trips and foraging trips, sometimes as much as six or seven miles or more from our house, often staying out overnight. You've read of some of those adventures already.

This experience with work horses seemed, in many ways, to be an extension of the previous experience except that Mike nor I did not handle these horses when they were "working" by pulling logs from the field to the mill. But we boys were certainly not intimidated by the scope of the work nor by the presence of these large bodied work horses. In addition, Mike and I were responsible for the care and feeding and watering of these work animals, those responsibilities then creating opportunities for us boys to gain the confidence and trust of the horses. A win-win situation.

OUR TOOLS AND TECHNIQUES

My faith and belief in God tells me that He was definitely "with" us every step of the way in all our activities, both work and play, at the sawmill. We endured about sixteen months of hard and dangerous work totally without serious mishaps or injuries. Within just a few days following our arrival on the sawmill site, Mike and I were exposed to those "tools of the trade." Our first job was to learn how to use them. While X was a short-tempered and impatient person, he was, at the same time, knowledgeable about the tools. We learned quickly, and with practice, became efficient in the use of the crosscut saw and the double-bit ax. In the beginning, shortcomings were our strength and endurance levels. The teaching/learning process was simple. X went with us our first two or three times into the forest area where trees had already been "marked" for harvest. With one or the other of us working with him, we learned to properly use the two-man crosscut saw and the double-bit ax.

THE TWO-MAN CROSSCUT SAW

Forest Rangers visited periodically to show us the current area(s) where trees had been marked for harvest. And it seemed to be my job to remember those locations. Having no power equipment (read: chain saw) we could cut down only two or three trees a day most days; we, meaning Mike and me. We used primarily what is called (as we learned it) the two-man crosscut. One of the things you learn about using a two-man crosscut saw is that you do NOT push. You only PULL. So, you must get synchronized! But young kids are almost always in a hurry so sometimes one or the other of us either pushed or didn't pull quickly enough, often resulting in heated arguments and "pushback" - so to speak. At issue with the two-man crosscut is that the users must, as just mentioned, synchronize their movements. Mike and I always began its use with the teeth barely touching the tree trunk to start the sawing "action." That is where we established rhythm. Once we were "in synch" we eased the teeth into the bark of the tree and began applying pressure as we drew the blade back and forth. Again, the basic admonition was that neither operator pushes the stroke, he only pulls the stroke. Pushing the stroke almost always resulted in the blade bending, thus causing it to bind thereby stopping rhythm, thus stopping the sawing action. The two-man crosscut saw was not particularly heavy, but was rather awkward for two small kids, because of its 5 or 5 1/2 ft. length and the large handles (handles made for big hands) on each end. Mike and I mastered it quickly however. Also, we learned right away that if we kept the blade oiled and sharp, and a steel wedge driven in behind the saw blade to eliminate pinching, (especially if we had any wind) we could fell a 2 to 2 1/2 ft. diameter tree in less than thirty minutes, unless, of course, one of us would push instead of pull. My recollection is that to harvest larger trees was fruitless because of the lower section(s) being too large in circumference for the sawmill cart.

THE DOUBLE-BIT AX

As I write I'm visualizing us at work. To attempt to make it appear in any way romantic or amazing or deeply interesting would be futile. So, I'll start with this: What it was, was hard work! A double-bit ax with a three-foot-long handle for boys nine and eleven years old was no small deal. (Note: A double-bit ax has a straight three-foot-long handle, i.e., not curved, and the blade fits on the handle to form a "T" shape.) The ax-head weight is perhaps 1.5 to 2 lbs. and the handle adds perhaps another 1.5 lbs. Both cutting edges must be kept sharp making it necessary to always carry a file and sharpening stone.

My body weight then was probably in the 60-70 lbs. range and Mike a little smaller. The ax would have been perhaps 3 or 3.5 lbs. So, proportionately, the ax weight was close to 5 or 6% of our individual body weight. Try working hour after hour with any tool which you must lift and swing that equals more than 5% of your body weight! Now, make a mental comparison of a 180 lb. man with a 3.5 lb. cutting tool. Quite a difference! In retrospect, an interesting outcome of just the simple (or seemingly so) task of swinging an ax to remove tree limbs from fallen trees and leaving no discernable "stump" of the limb – i.e. leaving a smooth surface on the main tree trunk – represents a considerable task, even for an adult. Mike and I became expert at that job and we could do it quickly. If we ever received praises from X, it would have been for that "expertise." Whether he complimented us from time to time is doubtful, but he might have. While the work was difficult and dangerous, we made it somewhat safer by keeping our axes sharp and in good repair making the danger factor less. This, thankfully, was at the advice of X as discussed earlier. So, we were constantly sharpening them, checking the fitting of the head to the handle, and keeping mud, dirt, tree sap, oil and grease and other undesirable things off the handle. Maintaining complete control of the ax was absolutely and vitally important.

Working in close quarters was not unusual and demanded extreme caution and common sense. Using an ax often involved making cuts close to the feet. And we were sometimes in precarious positions to cut tree limbs. I do not remember having footwear with steel toes. In fact, I believe we did not even have good quality boots or shoes. Therefore, we were surely blessed with a certain amount of skill, but probably more likely, a great amount of God watching over us because neither of us was ever seriously hurt during the use of the double bit ax. A two-bit ax head is sharp on both edges – no flat area. Care in its use is extremely important. A two-bit ax is not designed for "close in" work. Much space is needed to be both safe and effective. With practice, either Mike or I could cut through a six-inch diameter tree limb using only six or seven strokes. That assumes, of course, that the blade is sharp and well mounted onto the handle and the cuts are accurately placed. I believe it was after about two or three days of "practice" that Mike and I were then sent by ourselves into harvest areas. While Mike and I were both quite familiar with riding horses, (the word "riding" can be either a verb or an adjective) the horses we had at the sawmill were work horses – not for riding. While they were friendly enough, neither of us was big nor strong enough or had hands big enough to handle two or three sets of harness at the same time. Also, the "mechanics" of having a horse or horses pulling something, seemed beyond our comprehension.

Imagine two small boys, one of them a hot tempered red-head, the other one quiet and smart, getting along perfectly. You're right! We didn't! Note: Earlier you learned my hair color and my nickname. Perhaps those pieces of information will help you understand which of us was/is the hot-tempered one! We often fussed at one another, and sometimes got a little more than fussy! I guess sometimes one of us would "Push instead of Pull"! My sense today is that at that time we were probably overwhelmed with regard to all these new things we needed to learn. One thing that we for sure learned the hard way was to not get caught while bickering or arguing, especially when it kept us from working. This leads to my discussion, in a few pages forward, of the "walking stick."

FELLING A TREE

Before getting into the meat of this section, let me explain, in limited detail: "fall," "fell," and "felled." These are words commonly used in the lumbering industry. Here we go: A tree <u>falls</u> in the woods, but a logger <u>falls</u> trees in the woods. In past tense: A tree <u>fell</u> in the woods, but the logger <u>felled</u> a tree. As far as I know, "falled" is not a word, and "fell" is not a past-tense form in the causative sense. Hence, we will "fall" only the marked trees. Or, "We must <u>fall</u> at least three trees today." More elaboration is possible, but, in my opinion, it just adds to any lingering confusion you may have about fall, fell, and felled.

First was to make sure the work area was clear of anything that could impede our ability to safely limb and section the tree after it had been felled. This could include other trees, rugged, rocky or severely sloped terrain and wind (if any) were to be considered. The flatter the ground where the tree would fall, the better. So, to fall one across a ravine or ditch or across large boulders or stumps of previously felled trees was avoided as much as possible. Wind direction, in and of itself was rarely problematic. The force of the wind, however, had to be taken into consideration as to whether we would even consider falling a tree.

Once the decision was made about direction of the fall, a "notch" was then cut low in the trunk on the side of the tree that would be facing the ground after it fell. For instance, if we wanted the tree to fall to the northeast, the notch would be cut into the northeast exposure of the tree trunk. This notch had to be a minimum of about 35% or 40% of the trunk diameter in depth. So, for a 24-inch diameter tree, a level cut would be made to a depth of at least nine inches, then an angled cut starting four or five inches above the first cut is made downward to the end of the lower cut. That would create the "notch." Moving to the other side of the tree, we then cut toward the "point" of the notch at a slightly downward angle. Depending on the level of the ground, any impediments, and accuracy of cuts, the tree "should" fall in a northeasterly direction and land where you want it. Contraindications include: a tree that is heavy on one side because of disproportionate numbers or sizes of limbs must fall to the "heavy" side. Missing limbs are usually due to lightening or damage from a nearby fallen tree. Another would be a tree that is obviously leaning. It wants to fall that same direction. Leaning trees, however, were rarely desirable, thus rarely marked for harvest, since they often would have seriously curved trunks because mother nature wants them to grow "straight up," not "straight out."

Getting the most lumber possible out of a tree was a "rule of thumb" objective. However, of greater importance was the issue of safety. We were a long way from any sort of medical help, and we had no way of communicating with other people other than to physically go to them. I do not know for sure, but I believe the Forestry Department people intentionally avoided marking trees for harvest that were, in some way, grossly misshaped or otherwise not suitable for harvest from a safety standpoint.

Obvious malformations or situations were just that: obvious – meaning bowed or crooked or simply too difficult to access and remove. Among the most memorable things Mike and I experienced in falling tall pine trees, particularly those well-endowed with limbs, was the noise from the movement of air caused by this large mass of material falling and gaining speed as it fell. The sound was a sort of "whooosh" that gained in intensity the farther and faster the tree fell. Once we heard the first "cracks" as a tree began its fall, we only had to step back, leaving the saw in place so as not to impede our movement away from the tree, and watch, and hear the noises. The sound was for only a few seconds, but a mighty impressive few seconds for us boys early on.

This image was made in May 2018. The tree stump and top are within half a mile of the sawmill site. Judging from the degree of decomposition and the fact that the tree top remains is testimony of this tree having been felled for a lumber mill. It is highly likely that Mike and I felled it over six decades ago! It was probably twenty-four to twenty-eight inches in diameter at the stump which shows severe decomposition. Pacing the distance from stump to the remains of the tree-top, suggests that likely (three) fifteen or sixteen-foot logs were harvested. Finding old stump and tree remains, I believe is moderately rare, because most get overgrown by new tree and brush growth, particularly after so many decades of no lumbering activity in the area. This stump has a lot of rock around it and very little surface soil thus limited growth of grass and other trees.

LIMB IT AND DRAG IT

After determining the safety level of being around and working on a fallen (or "felled," if you prefer!) tree, our next chore was to remove the limbs and cut the trunk into sections. Each section would normally be 12, 15, 16 or 18 feet in length. Length was measured by using the ax handle and head for three-foot and one-foot dimensions. Mike and I learned quickly that this part of harvesting a tree was usually more dangerous and challenging than the actual felling of the tree. This meant we had to do careful planning on such things as which limbs to remove first and where to make them fall and then to remove them from the work area.

The highest danger factor was after the accessible limbs had been removed. At that point the main trunk of the tree was usually up high being supported by the limbs on the under-side of the trunk. On flat terrain this was, in the main, not a large issue. We simply hooked up harness and chains or ropes to the horse team to pull the half-naked trunk over, enabling us to safely remove the remaining limbs and then mark and cut the trunk into sections. After cutting the trunk into sections, chains and harness were arranged and the trunk sections were pulled to the mill. It seem we used a sled or skid device under a tree section to get it to the mill area. X always did that job. Mike and I were left behind to start on the next tree to fall or to finish removing limbs from and sectioning any remaining fallen trees or parts of trees. We harvested lots of firewood out of the tree limbs. Every few days before Winter's arrival, we took time to visit areas where trees had been downed and separate the dead wood from the green, cut all the wood into "stove" lengths and hauled it into the cabin area to dry while waiting for winter to arrive. Green wood at the high altitude dried fast, so it was ready to burn come winter time. The sound of tree sap exploding in a room stove was comforting music to our cold ears, so wood, still a little green, was good too! The smell of burning pine wood is pleasant and memorable. Mom liked the already dead wood for her kitchen stove because of a hotter and cleaner fire, meaning significantly less smoke.

Note of Interest: I watched a recent video on modern forestry that featured a huge machine, grasping and cutting a tree as tall as 70 or 80 ft., grasping and turning it horizontally, then cutting it into three or four sections while at the same time removing all the limbs and stripping the bark to bare wood. All of that work in the space of perhaps ten minutes! Then another machine was used to load logs onto trucks, which took another fifteen or twenty minutes per truckload! Amazing!

MAKING AND DELIVERING LUMBER

Occasionally, some hired workers were brought in when it came time to activate the sawmill machinery. Sometimes, however, X would work by himself. Neither Mike nor I was big enough nor strong enough to do that work. Though we did take care of disposal of scrap wood and made sure the area was kept clear of waste and, consequently, safer. For perspective, a 2 ft. diameter by 12 ft. or 15 ft. log that is "green," is heavy – several hundred pounds heavy. A heavy tool, called a "cant hook," was used to maneuver such a log. This tool was constructed of steel, with a stock of hardwood and was about four feet in length. Therefore, neither Mike nor I could possibly have done any of that work. X had to do that by himself or hire help.

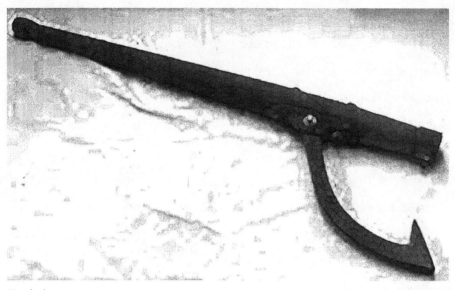

Cant hook

To underscore the value of the cant hook, visualize a stack of logs, i.e. logs lying parallel and creating a stack, perhaps as much as three or four layers of logs pyramid style. The value of the cant hook is almost immeasurable due to its relative light weight (for an adult male) and its design which allows a user to quite easily "roll" logs. The leverage afforded by the cant hook is its operative feature. A relatively strong 180 pound man can, with relative ease, maneuver a 1000 pound log and get it on the sawmill cart and cut it into boards. Green, or near green, lumber is heavy. Consequently, a truck loaded with fresh-cut lumber results in a heavy load. The road leaving the sawmill area crossed over a short, but rather steep, hill before entering a multiple-mile stretch of road that was mostly downhill from the mill to the lumber yard thirty or forty miles distant. The old 1930s International truck, by today's standards, was seriously under-powered. I have never quite understood this, but it was always much easier to get the loaded truck over that climb out of the sawmill area to the downward sloped road to town when it was driven out in reverse gear! Maybe it had to do with load distribution, or maybe a stronger gear ratio, or both. But whichever it was, it was certainly the way to get out of the mill area with a load of lumber. Neither of us two boys, as alluded to earlier, was big enough nor strong enough to effectively use the cant hook or the steel pry bars at the mill. Nor could we effectively handle and load on the truck the heavier two-by-six or two-by-eight, 15 or 16 ft. long lumber which were our most common cuts. Scrap lumber was thrown into the canyon or set aside, out of the way, for use as firewood.

Fresh-cut lumber was then taken, I believe, to the town of Cuba about forty miles southeast, and sold. It could also have been taken to Dulce or Chama, north and northeast of the mill. Only parts of memories of being on some of those delivery trips in that old International truck are clear. Especially clear, however, were some of the winter trips - because the truck had no heater. Mike and I had to huddle on the floorboards to get close enough to the engine for us to gain just a little bit of heat. Clothing we had brought with us from Albuquerque was less than adequate for us to be warm up in the high mountains in the winter at near 8000 ft. elevation. Thankfully, we did not spend another winter on the mill site.

One thing I was never entirely clear about was the finding and hiring of temporary workers. My guess is that they (the workers) found information on the locations of mills in the area from the Forestry Department and simply "went looking." During my early research phase I discovered that in the 1940s and 50s many sawmill operations were scattered throughout Carson National Forest – likely primarily in response to the nation-wide building boom following WWII.

FENCE POSTS FOR MR. DAVIS

On one of our visits to Ojito, Mike and I jumped at the chance to earn 25 cents for each cedar post we could produce for Mr. Davis. We believed we could harvest at least a dozen posts for him, so we quickly accepted the offer of that job. That then, became one of our first "business" mistakes. It is certain that many others followed for both of us!

Mr. Davis owned and operated the store and gas pump in Ojito. This little settlement is about 15 miles southeast of the mill site and on the other side of what is now Highway 537. And it is about 30 miles northwest of Cuba, NM. It was then, and is still today, a cluster of houses, sheds and corrals. Whether any of the Davis family remain in Ojito we do not know. We do know that the little town no longer has the store and gas pump, nor does it any longer have a post office. We learned that Mr. and Mrs. Davis are both deceased but that some of their family are probably still in the area. We also learned that Mr. and Mrs. Davis had thirteen or fourteen offspring. Maybe chances of some of them remaining in Ojito are pretty good. They had six offspring when we knew them in 1950 - 1951

The patch of cedar trees we were taken to for the fence post harvest was probably a mile or so from the Davis store and house. Mr. Davis took us in his pickup and sort of dumped us off and said something like: "Well guys, have at it!" That was still midmorning. When we were picked up late that afternoon, Mike and I were sweaty, dirty and very tired. And we had only four posts for Mr. Davis!

Learned in this experience include things like having the right tools all in good condition, i.e., no stressed handles, well sharpened cutting equipment, proper equipment, good gloves, good footwear, and protection for arms and other bare skin. But probably more importantly is a very good understanding of what you are harvesting! This mountain cedar was relatively hard wood we learned. If you've ever worked with green cedar, you know it is tough wood; it bends and springs, therefore it doesn't break easily. We wore blisters on our hands and got our skin and clothes full of those sharp cedar tree needles, finally managing to get those four cedar posts cut and trimmed after about six hours of work! Real business men we were - experience teaches!

WORK HORSES AND TRACTOR

In the beginning, we had the work horses to get logs to the mill as discussed earlier. Therefore, it was necessary that our horses receive the best care we could give them. So, after a day of work, the horses were watered at the Iron Spring down in the canyon (or good water if we had enough) and then brought back to their corral and fed. In the late Spring, Summer and early Fall months we could graze the horses on several acres of grassy land that lay south and west of the cabin area. Their corral was situated in a cluster of trees just northeast of the cabin area and they had shed-like structures to get under when rain and snow came. While Summer weather was relatively mild (we were above 7500 ft. elevation), temperatures would often be quite warm, so whenever we had the horses working we made sure that in idle time, water and shaded areas were available. The cabins we lived in were arranged in a sort of quarter circle with the one serving as the kitchen facing South, the next one beginning a curve in the placements and the third and fourth cabins completing the quarter circle, the fourth cabin facing east toward the canyon. The fourth cabin separated the third one (where Mary, Mike, and I bunked) from the horse corral. The best I can narrow down the time frame makes me believe it was a little after mid-Winter when one night we were awakened by loud screaming noises from the corral area and then the sounds of splintering wood and horses running. The corral area was only fifty or sixty feet north of our cabin, so we could hear the commotion quite clearly. We believed one of the horses probably became food for a mountain lion/cougar. Even though we searched several times, we never found them. We did see evidence, in the form of blood splatter and hoof prints, suggesting the probable demise of at least one of the horses. Sometime later, perhaps a week or so, we got the steel-wheeled tractor. It was a time-saver but more dangerous than we cared to think about and a lot less fun than the horses and not nearly as friendly. The tractor was a "hand-crank" start, so that wasn't a job brother Mike or I could do. Neither of us was strong enough nor tall enough nor heavy enough to turn that crank. Too bad! Further, neither of us could reach the foot controls, so too bad again! Often Mike and I would just look at each other and smile when X was having a hard time starting or operating the steel-wheeled tractor. I do not recall whether the tractor was diesel or gasoline powered. But I do remember that my job was to check the oil level prior to each day's use, and I was forewarned to not ever forget to do that chore. I didn't.

About the tractor: All the wheels were of steel. The rear wheels were, I think, at least five (5) feet in diameter and sported "lugs" (triangular shaped steel appendages to the wheels that gave the tractor traction) and they were not shielded with anything except a sort of "vertical" fender to separate the driver from the rear wheels. The drive wheels, then, were essentially bare. Being mostly exposed, those wheels represented extreme danger. No seatbelt. Nothing but the steering wheel to hang on to and a rigid steel seat to sit on. In retrospect, it was good that Mike and I were neither big nor strong enough to drive that thing.

THE TREATMENT PART
THE WALKING STICK

The bad part of our bickering was when X would come upon us during a confrontation. He always approached quietly, usually without our knowing until the last second or two and strike us with a long (about four feet) stick he always carried. This stick was about an inch- and-a-half in diameter. He called it a "walking stick." It wasn't a happy thing to be hit with it. Obviously then, it was much more than just a walking stick. Which is why Mike and I eventually agreed that we would search our surroundings for him before we began doing anything other than the work assigned – a measure made necessary by the "walking stick."

The other device X used against us was one of his leather belts. He had learned leather work in prison (as mentioned elsewhere and as I was told years later). He had numerous heavy leather belts, some with big buckles. Sometimes he used the buckle end. Whether either of us was ever cut, I'm not sure. But we were surely often bruised and scraped. I've since surmised that the use of the buckle end of the belts for punishment was because of the fact that Mike and I both, most of the time, wore more than one pair of pants at the same time. One reason was for warmth, the other reason was because we had few pairs of jeans without holes, rips, and tears. We wanted to be completely covered.

Other punishment, along with the striking, whipping, or imposed restrictions, was the verbal abuse that consisted mostly of belittling and profane-laced screaming and yelling. This almost always happened during his use of one of his belts. He never did that quietly. It is today even stomach churning for me to recall and write about those happenings. The result of the administration of punishment with a hand-tooled leather belt, for Mike and me, went far beyond the pain from the physical whipping or beating. In our minds, it clearly reached very high levels of dehumanization and degradation. And not too many years later, sister Mary experienced the same kind and level of punishment from X. Much more about this in chapter 16. While not a huge man, X was far larger and stronger than either of us boys. Being no match for him physically, all we could do was take the punishment and then live with the bruises and aftermath muscle pains, and sometimes abrasions and swelling. I suppose Mike and I both tried not to cry, but I believe we were always totally unsuccessful in that attempt. Neither of us ever forgot the pain of the language nor of the belts. Would a different tactic have produced different results? Probably so. Was he capable of using humane methodology? We don't know. I think it was never tried. Chances are he was raised the same way. I do not say that as an excuse, necessarily, just as a probable fact. This brings up yet another probability, which is the generational continuation of bad parenting habits and methods. So, I'll tell you a little about some of the parenting habits and methods Bonnie and I used.

DISCIPLINE FOR OUR CHILDREN

The example had been set. Mike, Mary and I had been whipped, hit, belittled, cursed, and disciplined in those and other harsh ways. Having just mentioned "generational behavior,"

I was driven then to question my own behavior toward our own children. They were born in 1959 and 1960, and at that time I had never considered the question about generational behavior, particularly as pertains to corporal punishment. So, I'm using this section to "skip ahead" a bit, but I'll return to our time in the mountains right after this short segment. As our children aged they were exposed to "family" television shows like "Leave it to Beaver," "Ozzie and Harriet," "Flipper," "The Donna Reed Show," and "Sesame Street." Bonnie and I witnessed, through some of those shows, a different set of standards for child discipline. I became acquainted with a whole new perspective, be it right or wrong, about child discipline. First though, I'll say that I am not now, and never have been, a great fan of Hollywood and TV personalities. But those shows did illustrate a different perspective on discipline and interaction between parent and child from that with which Mike and I had become acquainted. And I believe it later worked well for Bonnie and me in our own family. Being an entirely new concept for me, (I say "me" rather than "us" because Bonnie's rearing, in that perspective, was entirely different from mine.) reward/punishment ideas, was then, eye opening in the extreme for me.

To be sure of my next comments I had a conversation with Bonnie to validate my recollections about my own behavior during our child rearing years. I will readily confirm that I did, on several occasions, swat (with an open palm) one or the other of our sons at various times and in various locales following bad behavior on the child's part. And I swatted butts only, no faces, and no fists. At no time did I ever use an instrument (i.e., switch, stick, belt, fly swatter) to paddle either of our sons. Nor did I use profanity-laced yelling and screaming and belittling language. So, it would seem, God had stepped in for me again and likely enabled me to do little or no harm, either physically or mentally.

I believe, however, the most effective example I received for administering punishment to our children came from Bonnie. She too would lay one of our sons across her legs with his bottom in clear view and administer a swat or two or three with her hand. The number of swats to be given was announced to the offender beforehand, so he knew what to expect. I think Michael would count along with her, although I don't know that for sure. Sometimes, Bonnie has told me, when the administration of punishment was finished, the offender would get tickled and laugh. Then he and Bonnie would laugh together. Perhaps she "pulled her punches." The other related issue that I believe needs clarification was the type and administration of punishment Bonnie received as a child. To my surprise I learned that Bonnie had never been struck or swatted or whipped by either of her parents. She implied that any punishment she might have received would have been along the lines of not being allowed to visit or receive a friend or go to a movie or, maybe, not getting her nickel a week allowance.

She is a kind and gentle soul and that's how she treats all her friends and acquaintances, and me!

I'll close this section with this old saying: "Sticks and stones may break my bones, but words will never hurt me." Unfortunately, many people have grown up believing the message of that little "ditty." (My research on this quote revealed other versions of the statement, but this one seems most commonly used.) Simply as an editorial comment, I wish to refresh memory and information regarding time, place, and common ideas and attitudes of the time about capital punishment of a child. I offer these simply as facts, not excuses. Generally speaking, using a belt or stick or some other "instrument" to punish a child was not unusual, although most parents seemed to use an open hand to spank. Use of a belt, razor strop, or other piece of leather was considered acceptable. But using the buckle and metal belt tip rather than just the leather portion of a belt was considered "over the top." Additionally, for a parent/guardian to use a rigid material, like a stick of wood, as a punishment device was unacceptable. Now back to some discussion on our time in the mountains at the sawmill.

CHAPTER 10

The Daily Living

Behold the proud, his soul is not upright in him;
but the just shall live by his faith.
Habakkuk 2:4 (NKJV)

Whether we kids were "just," I don't know. What I do believe is that we, at least in today's world, would likely have been categorized as innocent victims. Suffice to say, X, being manipulative, plotting, and often cruel, was quite likely and in a twisted way, proud. Mike and I, in later years, talked about what appeared to be a "gleam in his eyes" following an administration of physical and/or verbal punishment. That his soul was not upright seems without question.

CONDITION: DEPLORABLE!

Candlelight dinners? Hardly! Cozy fireplace and a newspaper? Nope! More like kerosene lantern, smelly and smoky pot belly stove, and a bowl of pinto beans with cornbread for breakfast – if we had any at all. Listen to the radio? Nope, out of range of all radio stations. And, as alluded to earlier, we had no electricity on the property. Play table games? These were tiny shacks with no room for anything other than a bed and the pot belly stove and maybe a chair – and I'm not sure we even had a chair. As discussed earlier, we lived in four shacks, one of which served as kitchen. Next to the "kitchen" cabin was the one used by Mom, X, and baby DJ. The third was the "bedroom" for Sis, Mike, and me. The last one separated us from the horse corral and was used for storage. The kitchen cabin was off-limits for anything except meals and meal preparation. The sleeping cabins were just that. It seems the shacks were separated by probably 20 or 30 feet.

Because the land sloped downward toward the canyon rim, the shacks, by necessity, were built with space underneath to achieve (more or less) level floors. That space made the cabin harder to heat and would also become home for a variety of small wildlife that we could often hear at night. Whether it became a place of hibernation for some of the wildlife, I couldn't really say. But I doubt it because of human noise issues. The kitchen cabin had a side opening that needed to be propped up with a pole for it to remain open. None of the other cabins had any openings in any of the walls except for the door. So, if we wanted to be in one of the bedroom cabins, a light source was needed – even in daytime, although knotholes and much less than perfect fitting of side boards did allow bright sunlight to enter in a limited way. Being at an altitude of about 7500 ft. in New Mexico's north central mountains, we experienced cool and comfortable spring and fall weather. Both summers were warm and the one winter varied between tolerable and miserably cold. During those very cold spells often Mary Sue, Mike and I, in our cabin, would get the stove so hot that the chimney (stove pipe) would get cherry red all the way to the roof! These cabins/ shacks had no ceilings, therefore no practical way to "insulate" anything below. Heavy snow falls always resulted in snow entering our space below from around the stovepipe and through other spaces in the walls and roof. With a stove fire going, we got drips of water that would keep us awake from the hissing when the water hit the sides of the stovepipe or fell to the stove top. I've often wondered why it was that we never had a cabin fire. It helped, a little bit, for us to stuff paper and cloth into open knot holes and other spaces in and between the wallboards. After the stove fire burned out, which likely didn't take long after Sis, Mike and I were asleep, our "cabin" became cold quickly, because of that lack of insulation. The cold air could easily and quickly be felt coming through any open cracks and knotholes. Proof of very low temperatures in the cabin at night could be seen upon viewing frozen body waste in the indoor "potty". Unlike central Oklahoma snow, which is usually rather wet, snow at 7000+ feet as I recall, was deep and light and fluffy. Great fun for a while, then a real problem when you had to get work done and when the roads were trails of packed snow and ice. In retrospect, it is difficult to remember more than two, or maybe three, significant snowfalls. For certain, the temperatures seemed almost always to be at the freezing mark or lower for much of the winter months, snow or no snow. But I believe we did not experience a real blizzard.

One happier thing I remember about the winter months was when X built a large horse-drawn sled. It sported two bench seats, so several could ride at one time. Indeed, it was one of the rare "good times" in the mountains. When the weather was good, we were working. Meals were oftentimes skimpy. Cornbread and beans (pinto beans) were considered a staple, thus frequently served. Mom baked great bread which was even "greater" when we had butter and/or jelly. And when she had the "makin's," we got sweet rolls and pies. And all of that was done on a turn-of-the-century wood-burning stove! Meat was another thing. The best, of course, was when a deer showed up at an unfortunate time for its survival. To his credit, X always had the 30-30 ready and available. I believe the only time we got pheasant was when we left the higher mountains. Occasionally we'd happen upon wild turkeys. That was always good but with a wild taste and stringy texture. But we always kept a sharp eye out for <u>anything</u> edible! I believe Mom even tried fixing pear cactus, maybe baking or frying it, a time or two. It's possible, but I do not know for sure. Take that presumption with a "grain of salt" or a "dash of hot-sauce," if you wish.

WATER

I will give of the fountain of the water of life freely to him who thirsts.
Revelation 21:6 (NKJV)

High altitudes generally result in dryer air. Consequently, severe humidity is generally not a problem. One develops physical thirst a little more intensely and frequently in higher altitudes. When one understands physical thirst, then one can more easily understand spiritual thirst and how to quench it. This scripture explains the availability of the "water of life" and that it is free for the thirsty.

KEEPING CLEAN – A CHALLENGE

"Personal cleanliness" was a term almost completely foreign to us considering our means at the time. The primary problem was availability of water - good water! I mentioned earlier a water tank on a trailer. That's what we had. A tank. How to get it filled was another matter altogether. The little town of Cuba being about forty miles to the southeast, made it a day-long job to get the water tank to Cuba, fill it, and get it back to the mill site. I have no recollection of the capacity of the tank, but my sense is that it was maybe 400 or 500-gallon capacity. But since the tank was trailer-mounted, it was a relatively simple thing to hook it to the truck and load the truck bed with other smaller containers and have enough water for two or three weeks, or maybe a month in cooler weather. Bathing/showering was infrequent at best, and the "facility" was outside with just a canvas three-sided shelter and hose end. How did we shower with no running water? The water trailer was parked up a rise from the washing area, so it was a matter of gravity and strategic hose placement with a water valve at the end of the hose. Mom always stressed that we must conserve water, so I suppose Mike and I didn't particularly mind that, and it possibly resulted in us using less water. I didn't realize it at the time, but we did put into practice what I later experienced in my military life, which was the Marine Corps field-shower protocol: "Wet down, water off; soap up, water on; rinse, water off."

We did have access to the Iron Spring down in the canyon, but the water's hardness was barely tolerable, especially for drinking. The spring's heavy metallic content caused a harsh disagreeable taste in addition to its incompatibility with soap. The horses would drink the hard water, but reluctantly. And it was frigid cold! Just a "sponge bath" would turn your skin blue – even in the Summer months. Also, the spring's heavy metallic content would make your teeth hurt if you drank it. But that may have been more related to poor dental health and habits. The washing machine, Mike and I thought, was a mechanical wonder! Its little two-cylinder gasoline engine had a worn-out muffler, so it sounded "mean" and strong. So, we always knew when Mom was doing laundry. Therefore, we knew also to stay away, or she'd make us strip right where we stood so she could wash our clothes while we waited, standing naked, or near naked, until she finished. I do remember times when Mike and I had no clean clothes to put on while Mom washed the ones we were wearing. We'd put on wet clothes just to get covered up! And we were sternly admonished to stay standing - do not get in the dirt!

PLAYTIME

Most of the time, it seems, Mike and I were totally unaware of the day of the week and maybe even which month we were in. After all, at ages 9 and 11, and 10 and 12, we probably were not very much concerned about those things anyway. Possibly, the only time we were aware of the need to "get moving," was when we were told to. This was likely because Mike and I were never made aware of plans for the following day or week or month. Opportunities to experience playtime were severely limited, but when we had permission to do so, we quickly disappeared into the woods with our BB guns and sling shots. Or we may have used our "chunk-of-wood" car and truck toys and played in the dirt.

I am sad to say that I do not recall whether we ever invited Mary to play with us, but probably not. I am also sad to say that I do not recall any interaction at all between Mike and me with Donna, who was a newborn at the time we moved to the sawmill. My sense is that we worked so much that our playtime became more precious. It is probable that we thought things like: "What do you do with a little baby anyway?" It is also quite possible that Mom's message was that she simply didn't want two grubby little boys handling her baby.

NEIGHBORS

The closest neighbors we knew of was the Davis family in Ojito – where Mike and I made that one-dollar fortune cutting the fence posts. The trip to Ojito was almost never "pleasant." When we did get some rain, which was very infrequent, the roads turned to quagmires of mud. Therefore, a trip to the Davis' store in bad weather was always either a serious challenge or not at all possible. Even today the twenty-some miles to Ojito from the mill site has only seven miles of paved road. Since harvesting trees or running the mill in poor weather were not smart things to do, we would sometimes use the time to go to Ojito for groceries and fuel. However, in moderate to heavy rain, we dared not get out on the roads. So, rain essentially boxed us in for the duration because of the lack of paved roads. Refer to the 1960 map in the front of this book to see that Highways 550 and 64 passing through the reservation are paved, as is Highway 537 that connects 550 and 64. Everything else is dirt – that sticky "clay/dirt." And in 1950-51 Highway 537 did not exist.

While the Davis' were our closest neighbors, I'm not sure they were necessarily our friends – I mean in a visit over the back-fence kind of friendship, or "come on over for some pinochle" type of friends. On one of our food and gasoline buying trips, however, we were invited to "stay the night." The adults wanted to play some card games. Of course, X was always ready to play cards. Though, on this occasion it seems that no gambling was involved. It was, apparently, a "fun" night. Mr. and Mrs. Davis had six children, as I remember, three boys and three girls about fifteen months apart on average, the oldest being perhaps thirteen or fourteen. We kids must have been having a great time because around midnight the adults began their attempts to get us to "quiet down." Seems we were a bit noisy. This was one of very few "happy" times for us at the sawmill. This visit to the Davis family occurred in late spring of 1951. We departed for Oklahoma several months later.

Note: In my contact with Mr. Nelson, of Lindrith, New Mexico, during one part of my investigative phases, I learned the Davis family eventually consisted of thirteen or fourteen children. When we visit the Ojito area next time we hope to learn more about them and perhaps even renew an acquaintance. Also, of note here is that Ojito has had neither a post office nor a store for about the past forty years. The nearest post office is in Lindrith, about twelve miles southeast of Ojito.

CHAPTER 11

Visitors

…but God will surely visit you and bring you out of this land…
Genesis 50:24 (NKJV)

Because of God's promise to look over and guard and sustain us, it seems reasonable to believe He was looking over us four kids in ways we could never have imagined at that point in our lives. Today, knowing what I know about my relationship and my family's relationship with God, I am glad to be able to say to God, "Thank you, Lord, for keeping us healthy and delivering us from the sawmill."

SOME WE KNEW, SOME WE DIDN'T

More visitors we surely had, but my recollection is of only four visitors, or groups of visitors, that were of any significance to us kids. However, none, that I'm aware of, came to "take us out of that land." An aunt and uncle with Christmas gifts, an American Indian, Forest Service people, and the game wardens were the four parties I can remember with any clarity and specific interest. Other visitors could have been people with supplies of water or other consumables, people job hunting or perhaps wildlife hunters. In those years, many sawmills existed in that area known as Carson National Forest. So, seeing or hearing about a "stranger" being in the area, was probably relatively common. As alluded to earlier, I believe that most of the time Mike and I were totally unaware of time in terms of days, weeks, and months. That would be partly because of our young age, partly because of no sense of urgency or need to be someplace, no church bells on Sundays, doctor visits, friends to see, and so forth. However, we were also uneducated about welcoming visitors, so we seemed to sort of "go into hiding" when someone we didn't know came visiting. If we had any visitors following the Winter months, my memory didn't record the facts. My deductions are that the visits by "friends and acquaintances" we had must have been all at or near the end of Fall months, and early in the Winter. I recall that the Spring months of 1951 were very busy. It was also in that time period that (as I learned later) Mom had been taken, with Donna, to the bus station in Cuba so she could get to Pawnee, Oklahoma, where she came into possession of a car. More detail of this part is in Chapter 13 - Leaving and Arriving.

THE INDIAN

A great highlight, particularly for Mike and me, was when an Indian (American - In those days we had no idea about other "Indians.") on horseback rode onto our site one day and asked if it would be okay for him to set up his teepee and stay the rest of the winter. My assumption is that his arrival was probably late November or maybe early in December 1950. He had with him a second horse pulling, what I learned later, was a travois that contained his tent material and other "housekeeping" things. If he had with him bow and arrows or a spear, we did not see them. He did, however, wear a belt knife. In any event, Mike and I were much in favor of this request and made it known to Mom. We were so much enamored by our guest that we believed serious steps needed to be taken to allow this man and his horses to reside with us for a while. Our discussion and resulting actions went something like this: I said to Mike, "We gotta go ask Mom about this. And we need to ask her before we ask X." "Okay, but you do the askin'," Mike replied. When we approached Mom, she was fixing supper, the stove was hot and the "cooking cabin" was nice and warm, and she seemed to be in a good mood. Her response to the question was: "Fine, as long as I don't have to cook for him. But you have to ask X also and he probably won't let you." But to our delight X agreed that the man could stay. He did, however, make it clear to us that our visitor would need to stay away from the mill area. Also, Mike and I needed to make clear to our guest that he would need to provide his own feed (other than grass of course) for his horses because of our always limited supply of grain feed for our work horses. So, he stayed. And it seemed to please him a lot that he could leave his horses corralled with ours. He had taken down his teepee and left us perhaps a week or two before our horses were attacked; maybe he had a premonition. This Indian man said he was "about" seventy-two years old (so he was likely born in the late 1870s). His riding horse was twenty-eight and he'd had the horse since its birth. They just needed a safe place to stay.

During his stay he showed Mike and me his way of making a bow and an arrow from various local common hardwoods, and deer hide. He told us stories of fights he'd been in and places he'd been. His fights, he said, were more often with other Indian tribes than with white people. Retrospectively, I think he may have said that with a twinkle in his eye or maybe a wink! Unfortunately, Mike and I got to spend precious little time with him or his horses. One of my favorite authors is Tony Hillerman, an Oklahoman now deceased. Much, if not all, of his fiction involves Navajo characters and stories. It is through those writings that I learned about and to respect and appreciate many Navajo customs and traditions, particularly those regarding "family," that he revealed in his writings. So, in retrospect, I wish we'd found out why our Indian guest was by himself at his age and why he was not on a reservation. And I would have wanted to know about children and grandchildren. But I think mostly I'd be interested in the different kinds of dances and other ceremonial activities he participated in. And if we got that far, I believe I'd ask if we could see his dance costume(s).

Hopefully, Mike and I might have had the presence of mind to find out what he usually hunted to feed and clothe himself. Maybe he would have shown us how he made and used certain kinds of traps and other "tools" that helped him "get along" through his daily life.

I'm assuming he was Apache since the Jicarilla Reservation western boundary fence line, at that point, ran north/south in the shallow canyon area immediately East of the mill site. But, FYI, some maps prior to 1960 (or so) do not designate Carson National Forest boundaries clearly/accurately. Please see on page i, the 1950 map that does show those boundaries.

Back to our Indian visitor; he could have been Navajo because New Mexico's portion of the Navajo reservation was less than 45 miles west of the western boundary of the Apache reservation, i.e. westerly across the bottom of the western portion of Carson National Forest. Further, the Navajo territory extends west and north into Arizona and Utah and north of northwestern New Mexico into south-western Colorado. The Navajo reservation then, has within its boundaries, all of the "Four Corners" area.

For you readers who travel our nation's highways, if you haven't already, consider a road trip to this "Four Corners" area where you can stand at one single place and have a portion of your body on a tiny portion of four different states at one time! But a caution here: Consider going during Spring or Fall months because that point can be terribly hot in Summer and brutally cold in Winter. Bonnie and I know that as fact because we've been on that spot in 110 degrees of heat and negative 15 degrees of cold! It seems the air is always moving when you'd rather it wasn't and not moving when you'd rather it was!

RELATIVES AND CHRISTMAS GIFTS

Uncle Coy and Aunt Neva, still living in Albuquerque, visited us sometime just before Christmas, 1950. That's when Mike and I got the BB guns. We hadn't used them very much when X told us to put them away and not use them anymore. These were "genuine" Red Rider BB guns, the real thing! We decided we would hide them because we were afraid he would take them away and maybe ruin them or just not let us have them back. So, we went into the canyon below the mill and across to the other side, maybe half a mile or so, hiding the BB guns in one of the shallow caves. That location is on the Jicarilla Reservation property, not on Carson National Forest land. This was probably in February of 1951. Christmas time seems to usually remind folks of winter weather, and we had some. However, snowfalls, while frequent, were not always of high accumulations and would often melt and/or blow away quickly. So, adventures into the woods and canyon areas by Mike and me were frequent and easy to accomplish, even in the dead of winter.

THE SHOPPING, THE CHASE, THE GAME WARDENS

Major grocery shopping was done every three or four months. To do that required a day-long trip to Albuquerque to the south/southeast. At the time, the only closer town of any size was Los Alamos, which meant much higher prices for food items and a difficult trip due to its remoteness. Note: Los Alamos, in the 1940s and early 1950s was still a hotbed of activity around the Atomic Bomb development and production and was (seemingly) still populated with a lot of high-level government people. It was also extremely difficult to get to Los Alamos from the west as alluded to earlier. It is entirely possible we would never have been allowed to enter the town without proper documents or references, even in 1950. About forty miles southeast of the mill site is Cuba, which, in 1950, was not large enough to support a "chain" type grocery store like Safeway. I do not recall trips to either Dulce or Chama to the north. I believe that for Mom to agree to leave Mike, Mary Sue, and me at the mill by ourselves was unthinkable. That meant we three kids were (on the way back) crammed into the back seat along with fifty or one hundred lb. bags of potatoes, onions, and carrots and other purchases. The trunk in that old late 1930s Buick or Oldsmobile was filled with several spare tires, all likely with little or no tread and patched innertubes. At the start of one of those trips, X shot a deer on the way to Albuquerque, but not far from the sawmill site, and then shot a pheasant while near Albuquerque. It was a rule that when we were all away from the mill site, we took the rifles, the 30-30 and the .22, with us. It was with the .22 rifle that X shot the pheasant. Most bird hunters will take a second look at that sentence. But X was an accomplished marksman with any firearm. The .22 was "scoped" and he didn't have a shotgun. As he entered the car after retrieving the pheasant, he spotted a pickup coming off a side road and a "chase" ensued. I have no good recollection of how long the chase lasted, but he was not caught. It seems likely, however, the chasers got close enough to get the car tag number. It may be that's all they wanted. Mom stuffed the pheasant out the wing window somewhere during the chase. I can still envision Mom's opening the wing window and pushing the pheasant through it. I probably thought something like, "Well, so much for supper."

We picked up the deer as we returned to the mill area much later in the day. X just wrestled it up on top of the car and pushed it off in the mill yard. Early the next morning he butchered it. My thinking was that he was anxious to get the deer dressed out, salted, and stored quickly. This was probably because of the aborted chase after the pheasant kill – the chase abortion a sign that the car tag was recorded. About two weeks later we did receive a visit from two game wardens. Whether it was about the pheasant, I can only speculate. Mike and I were down the hill near the mill area, perhaps a hundred yards away, so we could not hear any of the conversation. It seemed clear to us, however, that X was not particularly pleased with his visitors. Looking back on this series of events, I've always had mixed emotions when I recall the "pheasant" incident because, while the kill was clearly illegal, the man was trying to feed the family.

FOREST SERVICE FOLKS

It seems reasonable to assume that Forest Service men announced their presence when they were in our area if only to be sure we knew the area(s) where they were marking trees for harvest. Also, I'm sure they wanted us to know they were around and for us to not mistake them for wildlife or "un-friendlies." I do remember the first time they visited because it was primarily for them to explain their schedules and areas where trees would be marked. The admonition was, of course, do not get caught harvesting unmarked trees! The marks were made with a single-bit ax blade on whose flat edge the raised letters "US" and the forest service shield decal appeared. Low in a trunk (three or four feet off the ground) bark would be chipped off and the bare spot imprinted with the "US/forest service" decal mark. I'm not entirely sure, but it would make sense that each tree was marked twice, once about three or four feet off the ground and a second at or near ground level. Thus, if a tree stump did not contain the US Forest Service mark, then the tree would have been illegally harvested. On the other hand, it could be that only a single mark was made very close to ground level. Those marks, however, would most likely be more difficult to locate.

1970 – FINDING THE MILL SITE

Years later, in 1970, Mike had been able to finally locate the sawmill site. He told me he had come into the area several times from his home in Colorado Springs to search for the Iron Spring Canyon area where the mill had been established. It was in Summer of 1970 that we met at the intersection of Highways 64 and 537, about twenty-five miles north of the sawmill site area. After establishing a campsite close to the highway and just outside of Carson NF near the area of our interest, Mike then led us to the mill site.

Mike was driving his trusty "four-wheeler" (a Jeep product) and I had my family in my company car, a 1970 AMC Matador. Access was by then unused lumber mill "roads" that were cut through the tan clay-based earth. Much of the road areas were overgrown with weeds and even some new trees. We just plowed right through them with Mike in the lead and me trying to keep up! I estimated that we drove about four miles off the highway before we finally accessed the actual area of the sawmill site. The mill machinery and all the cabins had been removed by then but even without the structures, the grounds looked very familiar.

One of our objectives was to see if we could find the BB guns. Sadly, we couldn't, but it was fun trying and remembering. We, at some point during that visit, commented about "not having any Indian trouble while on the reservation!" We were remembering, of course, the actual event of entering the canyon and crossing to the opposite canyon walls, thereby being on the reservation, probably illegally. I have learned that the area has a population of black bears now, something we didn't worry about when we lived on the mill site. If you should decide to visit that area of Carson NF, prepare appropriately for elevations of around 7500 feet, intense sunshine and air that is "thinner". Sunscreen and physical stamina are necessary to your well-being. The roadways today for access are essentially gas-well roads and traveled mostly by heavy vehicles, which often leave deep ruts. So, a low-profile vehicle is NOT a good choice. Also, heavy rainfall makes the roads almost useless because of the clay-based soil. Photos and verbiage in Chapter 8 will give you a better idea of the landscape. Keep in mind that those photos were made during good weather. When the rains come, those roads are not good places to be and it takes a while for the earth to get "smoothed out", hence, lower profile vehicles can be much easier used. Consider contacting the Forest Service office in Bloomfield to learn of road conditions and accessibility to the area.

About Forgiving

Jesus Christ teaches us to forgive those who trespass against us. I think most Christians know and believe forgiveness is necessary, not only for healing, but also to live up to our Christian faith by doing as Jesus commanded. I can say I've said the words, but sometimes I'm not sure about what is still in, or not in, my heart. I pray about it. Maybe that's enough, for now.

THE LORD'S PRAYER

Our Father in Heaven,
Hallowed be Your name.
Your Kingdom come,
Your will be done
On earth as it is in heaven.
Give us this day our daily bread.
And forgive us our debts,
As we forgive our debtors.
And do not lead us into temptation,

But deliver us from the evil one.
For Yours is the kingdom and the
power and the glory forever, Amen.
Matthew 6:9-13 (NKJV)

I do not dwell on thoughts of revenge or hate directed toward X. Rather, I feel a deep sadness for ALL of us who were subjected to his bad behavior, cruelty and dishonesty. Today four of us remain who were directly involved in most, or some, of these events. I am certain that none of us dwells on those happenings. Admittedly, however, an aura of discomfort sometimes invades our space when we are talking or thinking or writing about many of those events.

***

Part III
Work, School and the Trial

CHAPTER 13

Leaving and Arriving

...Jesus, therefore, being wearied from His journey,
sat thus by the well. It was about the sixth hour (noon).
John 4:6 (NKJV)

This verse clearly reveals the humanity of Jesus Christ.

I am sure when we completed our journey from The Sawmill to Pawnee, we must have had to "sit by the well" for a while too. This was a journey of some 800-plus miles, in an old car over two-lane roads with few, if any, bypasses around large towns and cities. I know the trip was made. But I remember none of it! Nor does Mary. It seems that Mike and I had talked about the trip in the context of how tiring it was. But we believe we were "given something" so we would mostly sleep. Nonetheless, we were very tired upon finally reaching Pawnee. And we were likely thirsty – in the physical sense! Thirst, in the spiritual sense, came later for us.

FINANCES AND PAWNEE

The question of finances seems important here. Part of the equation, I believe, is about insurance proceeds from the house fire. This issue was discussed earlier in a limited way. My comments now are a bit more pointed, yet occasionally also speculative. It seems reasonable to conclude that fire insurance was available through any number of insurance firms like AAA, Farmers, Allstate, Shelter and Liberty, as examples and to name just a few.

The premise then is: If insurance was a factor in the fire, proceeds from it were likely used to finance the move to the mountains. Then months later was a trip to Pawnee to buy another car. How could we afford to rent a nice house, get us kids in school, have food money etc. etc. when we got to Pawnee? And after a short period of time, X bought a property with a house on it and enough room for another building. Where did those finances come from? Did we cut down enough trees and make enough lumber to accumulate that money? I don't know, but it seems reasonable to assume or even conclude that insurance proceeds from the house fire in Albuquerque in 1950 and maybe some glib talk (X was very good with glib talk.) with some bankers along with some significant "down payment" money, would go a long way toward accomplishing those items. But back to the car issue. In Albuquerque the car Mom had was a two-door coupe. X drove the three-wheel motorcycle. I believe that the motorcycle was sold following the house fire and the truck was purchased prior to the move into the mountains. That left us then with the two-door coupe and the truck for our use during our time at the sawmill. It appears that plans had been underway for a while for our relocation from the sawmill to Pawnee. But we needed more than a two-door coupe for that purpose – thus, Mom's trip to Pawnee by bus and returning with a four-door sedan whose selection and purchase was most likely overseen or even accomplished by either Uncle Coy or Uncle Ward, or both.

ONWARD TO PAWNEE

We arrived in Pawnee sometime near mid-October 1951. However, as discussed earlier, planning for the move to Pawnee had likely begun about six months prior to our leaving the mountains. Communications would have been by mail and communication time was lengthened since we had no postal address except for the post office box at the post office in Ojito, those twenty or so miles away. And, of course, we had no telephone. I suspect mail was checked no more often than every two weeks or so. However, if Mom was expecting mail, the visits to the post office might have been more often than normal. We had accumulated another vehicle – a Willy's jeep – with a canvas top that was used to get around the forest areas when we were searching for trees marked for harvest, and it made our trips to Ojito more easily accomplished and cheaper as well. I made mention a couple of paragraphs back about Mom's bus trip to Pawnee and her return by car. That return trip had included driving through a strong and long sandstorm which stripped much of the paint off the car. Consequently, the car was already experiencing a good bit of surface rusting by the time we started East back to Pawnee. Luckily, it seems, the car experienced no significant damage to its "running parts" because I was told, when I asked, that we had no serious mechanical issues on that trip. At the time of the relocation, Donna June was about one and a half, Mary was eight, Mike near eleven and I was about twelve and a half. My recollection of the actual trip, permanently leaving the sawmill location, is non-existent, i.e., absolutely no recall of any part of the move from the sawmill in New Mexico to Pawnee, Oklahoma. In retrospect, it seemed to me almost like a time warp. In discussions years ago with my siblings we discovered that none of us had any recall of events on the trip between the sawmill and Pawnee, Oklahoma, in 1951. Suddenly, it seemed, we were living in a renthouse in Pawnee and wondering about clothes for going to school and which grades we'd be in. How? Laudanum again? It was still commonly available, cheap, and, as stated earlier, it works as a sedative. So, it seems to appear that Laudanum, or something similar, had been used on this and several other occasions of travel between the time of the fire and our leaving the sawmill bound for Pawnee, Oklahoma, most likely in early Fall of 1951. It is a disappointment to believe that these things happened, but, in all candor, not a real surprise.

WHY PAWNEE?

The reason for going to Pawnee was because almost all of Mom's closest family lived and worked in the area. This included her parents, two sisters, a brother, and their families. Probably the most daunting thing was getting acquainted and reacquainted with all those relatives! Mike and I had some recollection of our three male cousins, but we had seen none of them for close to two years and we weren't particularly close to them to begin with. But here they were: three male cousins and four female cousins – all right here in the same town at the same time! So, at family gatherings, which were fairly often for a while, one could count on a lot of noise laced with occasional and inevitable bickering.

The Renthouse in Pawnee, Oklahoma (Photo 1/20/2018)

OFF TO SCHOOL

School starting dates were very close to the middle of September and school had been in session for a month or more on our arrival. Pawnee is in farming country and in those days if a child was old enough, physically able and lived on a farm, he/she was generally considered to be part of the "hired help," so to speak – consequently the later school starting date in mid-September. I cannot help but believe that Mike and I must have been ecstatic about our different surroundings. To awaken to a morning of unfamiliar sounds and an unfamiliar room and bed was, at first, unsettling. But it seems we finally made the connection of this move to Pawnee to Mom's trip to Pawnee a few months earlier and driving a car back to the sawmill. Somehow the move had been planned, orchestrated and accomplished much to the joy of everyone except, possibly, X. I think it is probable that Mom had finally "put her foot down" and demanded a radical change from life on the sawmill.

Becoming acclimated to so many other people being around and having so many relatives that we kids didn't really know, seemed to just happen. And the practice of bathing (whole body - that is) more than once a month or every six weeks or something else, seemed, for a while, to just take too much time! But we got used to it. Getting reacquainted with traffic noises, music from a radio, other people being around, living in a house that had a furnace for heat, running water – both cold and hot, a telephone, and listening to radio broadcasts of music and news (it was a couple of years before we got a television set) were some of the many differences from living in the remote and high mountains of northwest New Mexico near the Continental Divide.

AGE APPROPRIATE GRADES SUCCESSFUL!

Mom worked hard with the school hierarchy to get Mike, Mary and me into age appropriate grades. The primary issues were: I missed school year six and part of seven, Mike missed fifth grade and part of sixth grade, and Mary (I believe) went into second grade directly passing over first grade. Donna June, being less than two years old, had a few years to go before school time, although I believe she was probably smart enough for at least kindergarten! Bottom line? None of us had to contend with being a year older than our classmates. Such a situation probably would not have bothered me in later years of life, but as a teenager, being a year older than your classmates would probably have been difficult, at best, to deal with. We all know how "thin skinned" teenagers can be today, and it wasn't much different then.

I remember some cursory kinds of testing that resulted in our being able to move on in school. It is possible, however, that Mike and I may have been required to accomplish some remedial studies to help us "catch up." Those considerations would probably not happen under similar circumstances in today's school climate. But for us, it was a godsend. We all did well in school and have (or had) no regrets with respect to getting in an age-appropriate grade when we finally arrived in Pawnee, Oklahoma in late 1951!

MATERNAL GRANDPARENTS

By the time of our having gotten moved to Pawnee from the sawmill, and we kids were getting acquainted and reacquainted with many of our relatives on Mom's side, Mike and I seemed to have been able to learn a little about relaxing. By that, I mean learning that our sawmill experience might be the last of our trials and tribulations. Maybe we would be living a more "normal" lifestyle. Well, that didn't quite work out. But here, I wish to reintroduce to you Mom's parents, our maternal grandparents, who had been living in Pawnee for a few years, having moved to Pawnee from Colorado Springs. I'll refer to them here now as "G & G" – so I don't have to spell it all out! Well, G & G had purchased a small apartment building when they returned to Pawnee and, I believe, insurance sales was part of what they did to supplement railroad retirement income. Their place was only about a block and a half from the house we rented at first, and when a house was purchased, we were just across the street from them. I do not recall much about interaction with G & G by Mike and Mary Sue, but I do remember some of mine.

One of the first things I believe Mike and I wanted to establish was whether Grandpa still had the car with the "Skull gear-shifter." It turned out he no longer had that specific car, but when he traded cars, he brought the shifter knob with him, so we could still watch it quiver with the replacement car transmission in neutral and the engine running! The house they bought was next door to the apartment building they had bought earlier. One feature of the house was a very large screened-in back porch off the kitchen. It also had a formal dining room and three bedrooms. The front porch, likewise, was large and shaded. Like most grandmothers I ever heard about, Grandmother Plunkett was a great cook! And it didn't matter what day of the week or month or which meal one might be thinking about, if you stopped at Grandma Plunkett's house, you were in for a treat.

This was the place where I became addicted to cornbread and buttermilk! Hot, hot cornbread in cold, cold buttermilk! Bonnie cringes every time I run to the store for buttermilk when she makes cornbread. Many folks like me, firmly believe that particular delicacy to be a required staple in any household! Mmmm good! Just as a last note in this section, I need to inform you that it was in one of G and G's apartment units that Bonnie and I spent our wedding night together. The weather was cold, we had no heat in the unit, and the bed was "short-sheeted." Welcome to the world of wedded bliss! Thanks, Grandparents Plunkett, and those complicit in this scheme! We both slept in the bus almost all the way to San Diego, fully clothed, of course! Can you possibly imagine a better way to travel when celebrating your marriage!? Neither of us had to drive!

JURY-RIGGED FUSE BOX

A false witness will not go unpunished. And
he who speaks lies will not escape.
Proverbs 19:5 (NKJV)

A lesson most of us learn early in life is that what goes around comes around and that we shall reap what we sow. Also, we learn that attempts to hide or cover up falsehoods are in vain, and that the liar will ultimately be found out.

One thing that has resided in my brain for years is the question of the etiology of the fire that sent us into such a radically different place and time and circumstance. Then, following our time at the sawmill, came our long journey from the New Mexico mountains to the hills of Pawnee, Oklahoma. I recollect bits and pieces of a conversation that I heard a few months after our arrival in Pawnee, between two of my uncles. Their conversation was about the question of why we had to move to those northern mountains of New Mexico since the house that burned likely could have been rebuilt. The part of that conversation that I distinctly recall included a reference to "jury-rigging the fuse box." What one of my uncles was saying seemed to indicate that he questioned if anyone had checked the fuse box because the fire, one of the firefighters had said, appeared to have started at an electrical receptacle in a living room wall. "Maybe a bad connection," the fireman had said. I am certainly not a qualified electrician, but it seems to me that a viable fuse should have neutralized a bad connection. If something other than an actual fuse had been used to replace a damaged or blown fuse, or, indeed, instead of a fuse, and a wall plug intentionally damaged or compromised… well? Factual knowledge? I don't know. Postulation? Perhaps. Maybe insurance money was the objective. At the time I made no connection between the fire and a "jury-rigged fuse box" until several years later (Mike and I were both in high school by then) when I saw X place something or do something with a pair of pliers in one of the fuse boxes in the hatchery he built and operated in Pawnee, Oklahoma. The hatchery contained perhaps a dozen or more large incubators (maybe 500-egg capacity each) and each one, (or maybe it was a cluster of two or three incubators) required a separate dedicated electric source. Therefore, we had a fused connection for each incubator, or cluster of incubators, and it was not uncommon for shorts to occur and "blow a fuse." The cause of these "shorts," I believe, had something to do with the automatic egg-turning feature of the incubators – that sometimes that feature would cause a circuit overload and "blow a fuse." So, when I mentioned "the jury-rigging event" to Mike, he replied: "Yeah, I know. He does it all the time." "You mean you've seen him do that?" "Sure", he replied. "Several times." My brother was a natural for things mechanical and/or electrical. He often spent time just tinkering with small gasoline engines and electric motors and devices. It was his favorite school subject, and it showed. When Mike entered the U.S. Navy, he trained as a Machinists Mate and achieved the rank of E-5 within three years. In private life he worked as a machinist, and at one point owned and operated a machine shop. His IQ, I believe, was somewhere in the stratosphere. So, I asked Mike, "Well, why doesn't he just replace the fuse with another good one?" To which he replied, "A piece of copper wire is a lot cheaper than a fuse, you know. But it's probably likely he somehow uses a heavy gage wire, or something similar, instead of a fuse because it won't 'break' as easily if at all." "But what about the reason the fuses are breaking?" I asked."Don't know", replied Mike. "I guess he's just too cheap, or stupid, or just doesn't care. Or maybe he wants another fire." Whether the fault was ever repaired, I don't know. Perhaps he <u>was</u> hoping or even planning for another fire?? Mike asked if I thought maybe that's what happened in Albuquerque all those years before. And we agreed about the clear possibility of the house fire being intentional. If X had a redeeming quality, it would have been his intelligence and his mechanical and electrical abilities. Food for thought. The question then arises again: Was the Albuquerque house fire intentionally set - to create circumstances that resulted in our moving into New Mexico's Carson National Forest where we lived and worked for those approximately 16 months at the sawmill?

———————————— ❋ ————————————

CHAPTER 14

More Work, Work, Work and God

But he who looks into the perfect law of liberty
and continues in it, and is not a forgetful hearer, but a doer of
the work, this one will be blessed in what he does.
James 1:25 (NKJV)

The etiology of the following phrase is unknown to me, and I probably even have the quotation wrong, but it goes something like this: "A day of honest work is good for the heart as well as good for the soul, not to forget the pocketbook." Mike and I, as you already know, started working at a very young age. So, I learned early the satisfaction that can come from a good day's work. I also learned about being "dog" tired, but still feeling good. And here I am today just having reached year seventy-nine and still working (at least if you agree that writing is work). I'm glad I can. I know, and know of, too many people in my age range who are physically and/or mentally unable to work but wish they could.

WORK AND RESPONSIBILITY

More work? Yep. More work. Was this work, in any way, for purposes of helping to further the word of God? Yes, in some ways at least, it was. We just didn't know that at the time. People around town noticed my brother and me and often commented on how hard we worked. Well, we had to get "spending money" somehow, since we arrived in town with none and we needed some. Thus, continued the learning of good work habits. And we suddenly discovered the appreciation and benefits of being financially rewarded for our work. We knew nothing of the Bible so we knew nothing about the book of James. But we did know about the relationship of work and responsibility. And we quickly became aware of the need to be responsible in our dealings with others. So, it seems we were possibly on the right track for understanding the Christian mindset about work and responsibility and the subsequent blessings. When it became clear that Mike and I still had work to do - even though we were enrolled in school - I think we must have looked at one another, shrugged our shoulders, and said something like, "well, fiddlesticks!" The rule had been laid down - if you want some money, you're going to have to go earn it because we just don't have enough to go around without everybody pitching in. After that pronouncement, we just grinned at each other and agreed that at least we might have a little money of our own for a change.

Here's something you may not know and which is possibly interesting to some with curious minds. A few lines back I used the word "fiddlesticks." Something made my curiosity factor question the actual use of such a word – so I "looked it up," so to speak. I learned the word is as an expression of disbelief, disgust, or even confirmation. It is also the name of a game or just an "all purpose" expression that can fit almost anywhere. However, the true definition it seems is that it is a name for a musical instrument used to add percussion and enhance rhythm with one or two sticks to old-time and Cajun fiddle music, allowing two people to play the fiddle at the same time, one using the bow and the other using the sticks on the strings at the same time, thus: "Fiddlesticks."

WORK WORTH DOING

We found pop bottles (no cans in those days) to sell, lawns to mow, trash to be carried, and lots of odd jobs around town. And our work ethics and habits continued into our adulthood and then to our offspring. And Bonnie and I are now in our eighties, and we are still almost always busy at something worth doing. I'm glad I love to write, but writing is not particularly easy as (probably) almost any writer will tell you.

Newspapers! We could deliver newspapers! Another family had the "Tulsa Tribune" routes all covered, but we discovered that the "Oklahoman" routes (Daily Oklahoman in those years) were available. All we had to do was drive to Cushing every day for the papers – a round-trip of about fifty miles. Mike and I started building routes and finding businesses that would let us place newsstands. But neither of us was old enough to have a driver's license, so Mom made the daily run to Cushing. It was all pretty good except for the fact that we had to make rounds each month collecting from our delivery customers. What a pain and what a disappointment in how folks could treat a couple of young boys just trying to make some money. This was when and how we learned about dealing with a few deadbeats. Happily, however, we encountered a lot of wonderful nice folks! I'm not sure which of us (Mike, me, or Mom, or X) came up with the suggestion that Mike and I needed to have some other way of getting around town and doing our deliveries and collections and newsstand maintenance, besides walking or waiting for a ride. Somebody suggested bicycles. With that suggestion, we (Mike and I) made our first "business investment" in a pair of very nice Schwinn bicycles, complete with front shock absorbers (springs) and a hand brake for the front wheel and a battery powered horn! I will not mention the name here, but one of the neighbors we had when we lived on Elm Street surely did become envious of my bicycle. When he complimented me on it and said it's "real cool" he was, at the same time, curious about how Mike and I could afford such nice bicycles. I presume my answer was quite smug when I told him, "We need them for business."

One day someone from the Indian hospital in the Pawnee Indian Tribal headquarters east of town, called, asking if we would consider bringing papers to the hospital. We were told that the patients asking would be glad to pay for them. We responded to that request, made a little money, and then decided to also take papers to the Pawnee Municipal Hospital. Our newspaper days continued into sometime early in 1954. As a note of possible interest, I recall the Oklahoman headline for an early March date in 1953 (actual date: March 7, 1953, a very cold morning in Pawnee) that announced the death of Russian dictator Josef (Joseph) Stalin. We ran out of newspapers at the stands and from our bags at the hospitals that day. Thus, began our work ethic and spirit that was ultimately beneficial in any number of ways for us both. During school breaks in the early spring of 1952, Mike and I hunted for yard work and other odd jobs; we were successful, considering that we were still just a couple of young kids. Additionally, we scouted all the roadsides for bottles and other glass, cans and other metal things, and anything else we could sell. Dear Reader: Are you old enough to remember when you could return your soft drink bottles and get paid for them? (In actual fact, when one purchased a soft drink the price included the cost of the glass container, therefore, when you returned a glass container you were paid for it.) And do you recall that common use of "power mowers" didn't come along until the late 1950s? It seems Mike and I lasted through two summers of cutting grass with muscle-powered push mowers.

By the end of my sophomore year, we were finished with the newspapers, yard cutting, soft drink bottles, and metal findings. We became involved in the hatchery and poultry business. Months later turkey farming started. Mixed in with all of that was a job as soda jerk for Mr. Lee Brock at the City Drug Store in Pawnee, which was my first "regular pay" job. It significantly added to the initial shaping of the education and work that was to come for the next fifty-plus years.

Some years back my mother sent me a packet of old records and pictures and a letter that said she needed to clear out her "file box." Included in the material are two W-2 forms of mine for years 1955 and 1956. In 1955 my taxable income was $672.50 – all from City Drug Store. That sum paid for 1345 hours of work - at 50 cents per hour for about 34 weeks. My 1956 earnings were less (about $600) and were divided between the drug store and starting up the turkey farm. So, it's confirmed – I started my "paid" work-life at age 16 at the end of my sophomore year. This does not include my time spent and money earned with newspapers.

To put some other things into perspective, it might be beneficial for folks much younger than Bonnie and I to realize that in 1953, television was in its infancy. A television set was NOT a common household item then. Our news came via radio broadcasts and newspapers – or just word of mouth. Entertainment came to us via radio, newspapers, books, the movie theaters, and travelling entertainers. In retrospect, then, it could be said that Mike and I provided a very valuable service to all our newspaper customers.

A PAWNEE SIDELIGHT

Across the street from the west side of the courthouse square and in the middle of the block, today, is the Dick Tracy Museum. A not commonly known piece of information is that Pawnee was the childhood home and birthplace, in the year 1900, of Chester Gould, the creator of the Dick Tracy comic strip. It is known that Mr. Gould, as a teenager, took an art course by correspondence while living in Pawnee, where he lived until 1916. After moving to Chicago, the Dick Tracy comic strip was released in 1931 and has been running ever since. So, it was that people in Pawnee in the early 1950s who subscribed to "The Daily Oklahoman" would read, certainly in the Sunday paper, but likely also in the daily paper, a creation of former Pawnee resident and Pawnee Schools student, Chester Gould.

Maybe we could have sold more papers if we stood on a street corner shouting about getting a paper today, so you can read the next segment of Chester Gould's newest Dick Tracy adventure!! Avid radio listeners of that era would also know they could catch the Dick Tracy show along with shows like Red Skelton, Bob Hope, Groucho Marx, The Aldrich Family and Blondie. One of my favorites was called, I think, "The Shadow." Seems it was a sort of mystery with a twist of deep dark secrets. It always ended with, "Only the Shadow Knows…" The Dick Tracy mural, shown on next page, is on the west side of the building at the southeast corner of the intersection of 6th Street and Highway 64/Harrison Street, having been placed in the late 1980s or early 1990s. Pawnee's Dick Tracy Museum is on 6th Street almost a block North of Highway 64/Harrison Street.

This mural is approximately twenty feet square. Note the rough texture of the side of the building

TURKEYS

Look at the birds of the air, for they neither sow nor reap
nor gather into barns; yet your heavenly Father feeds them.
Are you not of more value than they?
Matthew 6:26 (NKJV)

This scripture, in verse 27, goes on to discuss the futility of worry. Suffice to say, a custodian of a turkey herd must be, and remain, deeply concerned for the safety and welfare of his birds.

Up to about 10 weeks of age, the birds were housed in barns or sheds, so contrary to scripture, they did gather in barns! But not by choice. Then they were put outdoors, and their wing feathers were clipped to keep them from flying over fences. Water and feed needs were a twice a day chore. When they were mature enough (about 15 weeks, as I recall) they were put into fenced pasture areas with water and feed facilities. I'm not saying scripture is wrong, just that it is out of date, at least where turkey farming was concerned in 1956-57. So, obviously, St. Matthew just didn't know about turkey farming and that young domestic turkeys are just about helpless and quite short on brain power. They do seem, however, to have a certain amount of "wisdom," which seems somewhat contradictory. And neither Mike nor I was, at that time, very knowledgeable about God. But we were the guys feeding the turkeys! Conclusion? God placed us on that farm property to do just that!

THE INCUBATOR

It was early in our first full year in Pawnee (1952) when we became accustomed to a small incubator in the dining area of the house on Elm Street, and a fully enclosed bird pen in the back yard. It wasn't long before we had some ducks, geese, chickens, and turkeys in that pen. So, we always had something to eat! And every so often, more eggs would be incubated. Charts were designed, and notes recorded about hatching times and other necessary information concerning incubating eggs. Then one day things changed. The mood was different. Something was happening. It looked like things were getting better. One of those afternoons, when I came home from school, I found Mom and X having a conversation at the dining room table. I saw pleasant happy faces and the sounds were sounds of concern and interest and involvement. The reason for this big change was that we were moving. X had bought a two-story house on a large corner lot just a few blocks away.

THE HATCHERY

One day in late 1952, when I returned to the rental house after my afternoon paper route, I learned one of the reasons for the house purchase was its corner lot with ample room for another building. I also learned that the house was quite old and in need of much dressing-up and fixing. So, we spent most of the remainder of that year nailing, painting, trimming trees, and cleaning; in Fall of 1953 we moved. Mike and I were happy for the move because it meant we were through scraping paint and nailing boards and fixing this and that. We could get back to doing some things we wanted to do.

However, all that was to change again. Within a few months, a new building had been built on the north end of the property. This building then became the home for a bunch of commercial incubators. We were officially in the hatchery business. I cannot prove this, but the information I became aware of about two years later was that this small business in Pawnee, Oklahoma, was, at that time, the largest commercial hatchery in the state! It was also the beginning of our turkey business in Pawnee in late 1955. Pictured here is the 1951 Ford Woody station wagon, the first "company" vehicle used for the hatchery.

APRIL 1956

In early 1956, Mike and I were farmed out (literally) to a farm property about seven or eight miles west of Pawnee that had been leased by X for the purpose of raising large numbers of turkeys. Mike and I were to provide most of the labor for that enterprise. And we did. This meant that during the school year, we literally got up "before the chickens" (read: Turkeys) to feed and water the turkey herds. Yes, Herds. I believe the term "herd" was used for turkeys because once they got well beyond the "hatchling" stage where they were kept under brooder hoods and/or inside buildings, they were old enough to be turned out to pasture so they could graze in addition to being grain-fed, and they tended to graze in groups. Therefore, the term "herd." The first year, our quantity grew to over 50,000 birds! We always had large numbers of birds in each of about four "age groups," those being hatchlings, then brooder-house birds, then penned-area birds, then "grazing" turkeys. At the end of our first year of "turkey farming," the business cleared over $50,000 (a dollar a head) in profit. I never understood where all the money went, but Mike and I got precious little of it. $50,000 in 1955 was a small fortune. It was an easy decision to try it again the next season which began in late Winter, 1956. By the end of Summer of 1957, we were broke. That year was an extremely wet one in Pawnee county. Turkeys and rain, thunder and lightning do not mix! Thunder was the worst because it caused the birds to "stampede" and they crowded against walls or in ditches or along fence rows and other vertical obstructions where they piled up and the majority of the ones on the bottom did not survive. If we had insurance, it likely did not contain a provision that would have covered those losses. Either that or Mike and I were simply not given what should have been our "fair share." Curiosity, it seems, is part of a turkey's makeup. One might see a snake and wind up bitten, and maybe dead, due to the turkey's curiosity. In rain they will look straight up into the sky, and when rainwater enters their nostrils, they have been known to drown due to this strange action of curiosity. The other culprit we faced that year was predatory birds. Somehow, on one occasion, a broken windowpane in the large brooder house did not get noticed, therefore not repaired. This allowed an owl to gain access to the brooder house one night. It flew in and perched on a crossbeam near one end of the building. This caused the chicks under and around the brooders to "stampede" toward the other end of the building where they piled up. We lost upwards of 60 percent of the birds (perhaps 30,000) that season, which eliminated all profit and then some for 1956-57. The most notable memory of that time for me was that of neighboring farmers and ranchers coming by to complain about the odor of decomposing turkey bodies. We just did not have the equipment, and probably not the desire, to handle that problem. I think we apologized for that short coming, but if we didn't, I do so now. We were indeed sorry and disappointed in our inabilities to properly dispose of those dead birds.

Mentioned earlier was a note about Mike's mechanical aptitude and interest. One of his reasons for enjoyment as we worked the turkey farm manifested itself in driving and maintaining our small Allis-Chalmers tractor. But he also tinkered with it. One of those "tinkers" was to modify the engine speed settings by bypassing, or somehow modifying, the governor in order to achieve higher RPM's. Having some open fields and a couple of miles of dirt roads around the farm gave Mike plenty of space to drive fast. And he did. Smart? Nope! Daring? Yep! Fun? You bet! Lucky? I'd say so! How it was that he was never thrown off that tractor is a complete mystery to me. His only "anchor" was the steering wheel. So, seeing his butt completely clear of the tractor seat while bouncing down a rutted dirt road or across a rocky, and sometimes plowed, field was a real sight to see!

THE TURKEY FARM TODAY

These are images of what had once been a neat, clean, orderly and successful farm property. Mike and I lived and worked here during two seasons of raising turkeys commercially. Only one of the outbuildings, the barn, has survived – sort of. A workshop of natural stone walls (that served also as a bedroom for Mike and me when we had to stay overnight), has mostly collapsed. It was an attractive building that also sported a full bathroom and a propane gas connection for a small stove we used to fry morning eggs and bacon and other simple cooking needs for two teenage boys. The farmhouse in the lower picture was, in its day, a real showplace. And the owner had a new car nearly every year, usually a Nash, parked in a nice carport that is no longer standing.

What is left of the Blanchard house and barn on our leased farm.

Photographs: Summer, 2018

MUSIC AND COMEDY

As I prepared to write this section, certain memories of favorite radio shows came to mind. Mike and I spent countless hours working inside the hatchery cleaning, turning eggs, debeaking chicks, and numerous other chores, all the while playing our favorite radio shows. Of particular memory to me are those shows featuring Mr. Victor Borge, playing piano, singing, and telling stories and jokes. An American woman, while living in Denmark, married Mr. Borge. The marriage made it possible for him to gain an American passport which he used to migrate to the USA in 1940. He became extremely popular as a musician and comedian. Subsequently, part of his radio (and later, television) shows consisted of producing comedy from things he learned about "American" English language. One such act was his telling of a story of some sort that contained "oral" punctuation marks wherein, with lip and tongue noises, he would create quotation marks, question marks, commas, exclamation points, and periods, all of which one could clearly visualize while listening to his story. He called it "phonetic" punctuation. He also made fun of the dangling participle by saying such things as "I am learning about some things you do and say here in America, up with which I will not put!" Also, extremely popular in those years – just before Elvis Presley – were the "big band" groups like Les Brown, Tommy Dorsey, and, of course, Glenn Miller. My understanding is that while Miller was reportedly killed in a private plane crash near London during WWII, much of his band continued playing most, if not all, of his music for several years.

Then came the "battle" between Pat Boone and Elvis Presley. I don't know that we had "debates" in school about those two, but feelings seemed to run deep for some folks. Suffice to say, all these entertainers created and performed songs with real and understandable tunes and sang words that could be easily understood and (mostly) tolerated by the American public. Of course, Presley's physical gyrations onstage were often subject to criticism. However, his were songs of hopes and dreams and love and unladen with sexual inuendo. To be sure, however, we had a lot of upbeat music that was fun and energetic and acceptable for any age group and many belief systems. Probably, just to illustrate my age, I guess, I'll reveal to you that my favorite tune of all time came via the Glenn Miller orchestra and was called "In The Mood." I'll be humming that tune for the next several pages of writing I expect!

THE SODA JERK

Unlike Job, who in Chapter 7 of the book of Job laments his hard work of service as a hired man, my approximately 14 months of work as a soda jerk in the City Drug Store working for Mr. Lee Brock and Mr. Don Chadwick is what interested and propelled me into the world of pharmacy". Don was then enrolled in the pharmacy school program in Weatherford, OK but was working the store during session breaks and Summer break.

(Unfortunately, Don lost his life in a car crash about a year later as he was returning to Pawnee from school in Weatherford.)

Immediately, following the failure of our turkey venture, my job at City Drug Store became full time. This was when I began learning much more about working with other people and serving customers. I also learned about balancing my time between school and work. It was near the end of my senior year at Pawnee High. My birthday is near the end of May, which was always exciting for me because my birthdate was always on or very near the last day of the school year! Some years I probably accepted the "last day of school" as a legitimate birthday gift.

Because I had begun to take a deeper interest in "girls" in my Junior year, I found that spending money ("spending" in this context is an adjective, not a verb) also known as "pocket money", was a little bit more important. Also, I had acquired my first car. It became required then, that I have some income besides lunch money. It has never become clear to me what exactly caused me to fill out a work application for the City Drug Store, but much to my amazement one day, a note was delivered to me at school that said to get in touch with Mr. Lee Brock at the City Drug Store. That's when I officially became a "soda jerk." Starting pay for a job behind a soda fountain was something like 25 or 30 cents per hour. That meant I could accelerate my payment schedule for the car I bought about a year earlier. I had purchased a 1949 two-door Chevrolet coupe for 300 dollars and my payments were 10 dollars per month. How nice! Also, having a bit of "regular" money heightened my courage to ask girls to go on dates. So, I did.

However, in those years (and probably today as well) when you are a small guy, not a football player, a guy who makes very good grades, a church goer most Sundays, redheaded with freckles, and who owns a two-tone gray old (1949) Chevy two- door with glass out of the right-side door and six or seven spare tires in the trunk and back seat, the ability to get dates is seriously reduced. I dated only two girls before dating Bonnie. One was two or three inches taller than I, which seemed to not work out very well. The other, on our second or third date conceded to a kiss, but it was actually I who conceded. I think she scared me off. Then I met Bonnie. The rest, as they say, is history. I was blessed with great luck, and I proved (to myself at least) that persistence pays off. Bonnie was then, and still is, no pushover! I met and dated the love of my life in high school! It turned out to be an extremely good thing. I never made it to college, but Bonnie's help, even with a newborn and an eighteen-month-old to care for, was very instrumental in my successful completion of the year-long Pharmacy Tech school program at the U.S. Naval Hospital in San Diego. We have a small bunch of grandchildren and great-grandchildren. We celebrated our sixtieth wedding anniversary in late October of 2018!

SODA JERK TO PHARMACY TECH

My motivation to apply for and receive my appointment to the U.S. Navy Hospital Corps Pharmacy School in San Diego, California, in my second year in the U. S. Navy began with my experience at the City Drug Store in Pawnee. At some point fairly early in that job, I began to imagine myself wearing a white coat or smock and working behind a glassed-in pharmacy section of a drug store. Thus, my motivation and hard work in completing my pharmacy training in the Navy. But, back to my time at the drug store in Pawnee. Being a "counter guy" and "soda jerk" were not my only experiences at the City Drug Store. I also got to clean up and rearrange furniture and put other things in their proper places at closing time when I would work on Friday and Saturday evenings. I believe having to do those things helped me realize that the small things count too. But I bring this up to add another "tidbit" to this story; a tidbit that I've had fun with for many years. My rationale for injecting the following is primarily to illustrate the fact that "we kids" have all been able to maintain realistic life views. Each one of us has, I believe, also used humor to help deal with much of the fallout of our experiences involving X. Mike was a great one to poke humor at himself and, for that matter, anyone else close by. It seems that all of us siblings have or had been able to use and enjoy humor as a vehicle to get on with our lives. So, here is one of the stories I use for that purpose. Enjoy!

THE DRUG STORE TABLE TOP

This Saturday evening in Pawnee, in July or August of 1957 was hot and muggy. It was about three or four months prior to my leaving Pawnee to join the U. S. Navy in San Diego, California, in November. My spirits were high. But the miserably muggy evening wasn't over as we had yet to deal with the "movie crowd" from the theater next door. They would shortly come piling in looking for ice cream and cold drinks and making a lot of noise. Part of the problem was that this business, like most others in town, was not air conditioned. Neither was the movie theater I believe. That was good for us because everybody wanted something COLD after the movie. The other problematic issue was the abundance of mosquitos and flies. Pawnee, being a farming community, had its share of those pests. While we had ceiling fans to help against the heat, we also had screen doors (so we could leave the glass-panel front doors open) to help with air circulation.

Well, finally, here came the movie patrons looking for that ice-cold drink or the cold smooth and creamy vanilla, chocolate, or strawberry ice cream concoctions. The crowd was in and out and in and out with the screen doors flapping endlessly, letting, we believed, every fly and mosquito in the country inside the store. And then the crowd was no more. We were finally getting ready to close. While Mr. Radley took care of closing the pharmacy part, the rest of us began moving chairs and tables out of the way, sweeping and mopping. And swatting flies. Finally, things seemed under control and we began preparing to lock the doors and leave. With my arms full of mops and brooms, I was headed for the utility closet when I saw another fly. Drat! It was on one of the tabletops.

The furniture was, and still is, booth sets (bench seats with rectangular tabletop between) and small circular-topped tables with triangular seats that fit around and under each table, four seats per table. All tabletops, both circular and rectangular, were of faux marble material. It was on one of those round tabletops that I spotted that big black fly. A big horsefly. Couldn't miss it, I thought, raising one of the straw brooms. I took a swing at the fly and got it! But I also broke the tabletop! It broke into two nearly equal halves. Don Chadwick, being in charge that evening, calmly took control of things, and directed us to gather up the broken tabletop and base, and the four chairs, for storage in the attic space. Don was on a school break and always worked when he could. As mentioned earlier, Don lost his life in a car crash just a few months later.

Immediately following my agreed upon termination date of October 31, 1957, from City Drug Store, I entered the U.S. Navy and trained as a Hospital Corpsman. A couple of years later, I graduated from the very long Pharmacy School program. It was necessary for me to extend my enlistment for two years so I would actually be able to work as a Pharmacy Tech after training. After ten and a half years of Navy time, I did not reenlist, but chose instead to join a pharmaceutical firm as a sales representative (called "detail men" in those years. Women began entering that business a few years later). I was promoted to a district management slot out of Oklahoma City after working several years as a market researcher, following nearly five years in the sales department.

My district included all of Oklahoma and parts of each surrounding state with sales reps in the major metro areas. One of the Tulsa-based sales territories included Pawnee. Each District Sales Manager was required to have group sessions from time to time, and we were asked to make them as enjoyable and interesting and as informative as possible. My Tulsa sales representative, I'll call her Rhonda, since that was her name, had been able to work closely with Mr. Radley, who had purchased City Drug Store from Mr. Brock sometime close to 1965. As Rhonda developed her territory following a district reorganization, she developed a good working relationship with Mr. Radley. I had been assigned to this sales district in 1969 but was unaware of Mr. Radley's ownership of City Drug Store until my own visit to the store while circulating through my district soon after being assigned as District Manager. (By the way, I'm still humming "In The Mood"!)

Pawnee, being within the geographic center of my district, seemed a good choice for a place to hold a district meeting. An attractive feature of Pawnee is the Pawnee Bill museum and ranch grounds which have space and facilities for gatherings. So that's where I set this one up. As we approached our time to close the meeting, my senior sales rep asked me to join him in front of our group. Then he called on Rhonda, asking her to come forward. The wrapping of the package she carried suggested something a little bit large, and the way she carried it suggested a little weight. As I received it, and with Rhonda's assistance, began removing the wrapping, I noted the heaviness and shape of the content. I could not conceal my surprise and pleasure on viewing the package content. It was, indeed, one half of the tabletop from City Drug Store! Jim Radley, whom I hadn't seen or talked with for something like eighteen or nineteen years had taken ownership of the drug store some fifteen years earlier. Rhonda explained to me, and to the rest of the team, the story behind the one-half tabletop leaving nothing to the imagination.

While Rhonda was complicit in this gift giving, its genesis was one Mr. James Radley, practical joker emeritus and general class clown. So, I believe I was correct in accusing Rhonda, in front of the whole team, of conspiracy; conspiracy in the highest order! After our meeting was over, I drove to City Drug Store to personally thank Mr. James Radley for this awesome and wonderful and thoughtful gift.   It indeed was a pleasant surprise! But what was I going to do with it? I'm a fairly good woodworker, so I figured out a plan and completed it. That one-half tabletop with the broken side now cut straight with my tile saw, is now fitted into a small vanity type shelf mounted on the side of our stairwell. That stair-sidewall faces the main entryway and front door of the house and provides enough wall-space to mount the small cabinet, whose top is my portion of the tabletop. It is quite attractive and captures some attention from visitors. That is when I get to talk about it and tell this story! How nice!

It was my working relationship with Mr. Radley back in 1957 that prompted me to first train as a Navy Hospital Corpsman and several months later, after hospital and clinic work, apply for and receive appointment to Pharmacy School. During my next several years of working in the pharmacy world "practicing" pharmacy, I became friends with "detail men" (Pharmaceutical Sales Reps) from a wide variety of pharmaceutical firms who called on me (and the other pharmacy techs, as well as, our departmental pharmacist). It was the influence of these relationships that prompted me to seek a position as a sales rep with a pharmaceutical firm. I am proud of that success, and the opportunities it has afforded me in many other things I've been able to accomplish.   Finally, considering all the things my siblings and I endured in our early lives, I thank the Lord for all the opportunities He has given us to achieve good and proper and honest things and activities in our lives. All four of us married, raised families and did honest and honorable work. I conclude this interruption by acknowledging that God, somehow for me, played a part in my splitting into two pieces a drugstore ice cream parlor, faux marble tabletop from the early 1900s, for His own reasons.

The wood is stained and clear-coated red oak. We keep keys, a small flashlight and an emergency whistle in the drawer. Mounting brackets are concealed under the removable "one-half" tabletop.

The triangular chair pictured above is now refinished and painted bright red. Its station is directly under the entryway shelf and drawer. At this writing I'm hopeful of obtaining one of the booth and table sets, but I'm not holding my breath.

CHAPTER 15

Bonnie, The Love of My Life!

*Ask and it will be given to you; seek and you will find; knock
and it will be opened to you. For everyone who asks receives and he who
seeks finds and to him who knocks, it will be opened.*
Matthew 7:7 (NKJV)

Miracles do happen. Perhaps better stated: God's grace is infinite and powerful! The fact that Bonnie and I married when we did, and under less than good circumstances, coupled with the fact that this year we have entered our seventh decade of marriage, is testimony enough to declare the longevity of this marriage almost miraculous! Not only did our marriage survive, it thrived. Our love for one another not only survived, it grew. These things happened in spite of many adversarial circumstances, some being the kinds that destroy marriages. The worst of these was the suicide death of our older son, Michael, in 1991. God has, indeed, graced our marriage with blessings of enduring love and profound respect, and increasing strength.

ANCHORS AWEIGH, MY BOY!
A SLUGGISH BEGINNING

The following is a synopsis of happenings and circumstances after our high school graduation, some of which could have scuttled almost any matrimonial intentions. Immediately following graduation, Bonnie moved to Eldorado, Kansas, to help a sister-in-law care for her children while preparing for the birth of another. In the meantime, I continued working for Mr. Brock. I desperately wanted to marry Bonnie and made two trips to Eldorado to ask her to accept an engagement ring. But she wouldn't. We continued writing letters and I was still working for Mr. Brock. We had both graduated high school in May of 1957.

One day in early October 1957, I was visited by a Navy recruiter who convinced me to enter the U.S. Navy, which I did in late November. I have no recollection of bidding farewell to Bonnie or my siblings, although I probably did. I learned later that this visit from the Navy recruiter was "set up." Whether by Mom or X, I was not sure until my sister Donna said in a recent email to me that Mom was involved in getting the Navy recruiter to "visit" me. My suspicion, recently confirmed, is that Mom wanted both of us boys away from home for reasons I was not clear about at that time but which, obviously, had to do with what she knew, or thought, X was doing. Following Boot Camp was Hospital Corps School. Then came duty at the Naval Hospital, San Diego. My brother Mike and I met after his Boot Camp training, his having joined the Navy "under duress" in early 1958. He did not graduate high school but achieved a GED certificate. In October 1958, I was working in a Neurosurgery Ward at San Diego Naval Hospital when I received a message to "call home." I was needed in Pawnee to testify in court against X.

A little over a year had passed since I had seen Bonnie. We had been writing but had had no discussions by phone because that was too expensive!

I had learned she was staying with Mom in Pawnee, but I had no detail about that situation. I was extremely anxious to see her. We had already made the decision to marry (by U.S. Mail) but had not discussed any details. I have little recollection of our discussions once I was in Pawnee, but we ultimately decided to make the best of a bad situation and get married as soon as possible after the trial.

Bonnie and I were married in the First Christian Church of Pawnee, Oklahoma, in the early afternoon of October 29, 1958. And we have not looked back! Two days later we were aboard a bus out of Tulsa, Oklahoma, for the journey to San Diego, California, that took parts of three days. We were looking forward to our future! Our first home was a shared rental house on a quiet street off University Avenue in San Diego with our friends Mac and Linda and their baby daughter. All our belongings were in a small trunk, a kind of civilian footlocker. And we had no car. The neighborhood we lived in was not far from the Naval Hospital, so we did not really need a car. I always walked to the hospital rather than spend money on bus fare. One of the nice things about walking was that the path went alongside the San Diego Zoo which was (and is) laden with all sorts of plant life. The aroma from the flowers, almost year-round, was (and is) outstanding and memorable. At some point small conflicts began to crop up, and we found it necessary to make other living arrangements rather than lose a friendship. Mac and Linda kept the little house, and Bonnie and I went apartment hunting. All we had was our small trunk of clothes and my Navy gear and clothing. At the time it was fairly easy to find small furnished duplexes or cottages or apartments, so we would rent one for a month or two and then find another. By then Bonnie was pregnant with Michael, and I was accepted for Pharmacy School. We had settled on a nice little quadraplex. That's when we met Flo!! As it turned out, we were off to a great start!

FLO

I introduce Flo to you because she was a big part of our lives during Bonnie's pregnancy with Michael, our firstborn, and his "babyhood." Flo worked as an aircraft mechanic for the civil service at one of the many military establishments around San Diego. I worked in a nursery unit near the delivery rooms of San Diego Naval Hospital. My job was to package and autoclave everything from baby formula to surgical caps and gowns to surgical instruments. The exact type of work Flo did I am unclear about, but it had something to do with maintenance of aircraft control systems. Flo looked very old to Bonnie and me, but she was probably only about forty-five or so. Being a mechanic, she always sported soiled hands and dirty fingernails and unkempt hair and smelled like oil and grease and smoke. Flo chain-smoked unfiltered Camel or Chesterfield cigarettes. The cigarette smell didn't bother me because I also smoked at the time. And I guess Bonnie was accustomed to it, or said she was, by that time.

Flo was a sweetheart! The first thing Flo did for me was to teach me the game of cribbage. I can say today that I'm a very good cribbage player as is my younger son, Robert. See how that works? (Note: Robert and I are, today, still involved in local cribbage activities. We played just last night and both of us failed to place. Oh well, next Monday evening is only six days away!) Then Flo turned her attention to Bonnie and baby. By the time Michael was born and brought home, Flo had outfitted him with a baby bed, a stroller, a swing set, a highchair, and a bathtub! Then Flo seemed to turn her attention back to me and cribbage. She was a relentless teacher of the game, and she extended no favors. I believe I must have celebrated the first time I won more than one game in a row. Well, maybe it was when I lost only two or three games in a row. As Bonnie and I talked about her during this writing, we could not help but recall how difficult it was for us to refuse Flo when she asked if she could babysit during times when we both needed to be someplace else. The reason for the refusal was that Flo had a drinking problem. And that, coupled with her aggressive smoking habit, signaled the potential for serious trouble. We always made sure to refuse the help in a kind and dignified way. Sometimes, I suppose, with a little "white lie" attached. By the time of Michael's birth, I had been accepted for and started pharmacy school, so I had precious little time to spend with our newborn. We did, then, give plenty of opportunities for Flo to be involved with Michael. Right after pharmacy school graduation I received orders to report aboard the USS Prairie (AD-15) for sea duty and independent pharmacy duty beginning 1 January 1961. And, by then, we had another member of our small family — Robert, born on November 2, 1960.

CHAPTER 16

The Victim / Witness / Trial

I broke the fangs of the wicked and plucked the victim from his teeth.
Job 29:17 (NKJV)

X's "fangs" went deep into all who had trusted in him and, certainly, into my sister, Mary, who has experienced the difficulties of a hard struggle to regain a semblance of normal life; even to the point where she can, in a calm way, talk about that part of her life. The "fangs" were broken when X was arrested, tried and convicted, and sent to prison. Praise God! None of us involved in the arrest, trial and/or conviction almost sixty years ago have seen him since.

Pawnee County Court records reveal that twenty witnesses, seven for defense and thirteen for prosecution, were called during the three-hour trial. My testimony, as revealed later in this chapter, was brief, lasting only a few minutes. Mary's, predictably, was much longer. She recently said it seemed to last for "hours." Our brother Mike, I am given to understand, was not available because his ship was at sea. Aircraft carriers seem to rarely be in port. I have seen the roster of witnesses, but I knew only one or two outside of family. The names I knew were not friends of mine, but probably Mom's friends. Whether any were friends of my sister, I do not know. I spoke with Mary during this specific writing, but we have, so far, made no journey into details of her time on the witness stand. Maybe later. Sister DJ was age eight at that point and would not have been called to testify on either side, I am sure. As noted elsewhere, the phone call to be a prosecution witness was by way of my mother to someone of authority in the Personnel Office of the San Diego Naval Hospital. I was summoned from my workstation (at that time in a Neurosurgery Ward) to report to the base personnel office. It was then explained to me that Mom had called and was requesting my presence during X's trial which would be in just a few days. Mom apparently leaned hard because I had no trouble gaining permission for emergency leave. However, the Chaplain, who was required to "sign off" on the permission papers complained loudly to me about people who seemed to not be able to live problem-free lives. Or something like that. I looked at him and said, rather pointedly, "Thank You, Sir," and I left for the bus station. The essence of my testimony appears later in this chapter. I boarded a bus in downtown San Diego bound for Oklahoma City and Tulsa. Long distance highway travel in the 1950s, because of the lack of completed interstate highways, was considerably slower than it is now. A 1600-mile trip, as it was from San Diego to Oklahoma City, meant something like forty or more hours of "straight-through" drivers driving in relays. As I observed them, the oncoming relay driver was waiting at the planned meal-stop location and would do his pre-trip inspection and fuel the bus while the passengers were having snacks or a meal. At his announcement, we passengers re-boarded and were on our way again. I think it was in Santa Rosa, New Mexico, when I failed to be on the bus before it left. A small "ditty" bag (that's a Navy provided "incidentals" bag) was all I carried, and I had taken it into the bus terminal where we could eat and take care of personal needs. Having attended to those things, I bought a candy bar and headed toward the bus which I watched as it left the parking area headed for the highway (Highway 66), bound for Oklahoma City with a stop in Amarillo. Well. What now? I had never "hitch hiked" before, but I was heads up enough to know I needed to try it now. Stories I had heard or read concerning the perils of hitching a ride with an unknown person came to mind as I stuck out my thumb. But common sense seems to have convinced me that I should try anyway. I did catch a ride just a few minutes after putting my thumb out. It seems the uniform probably helped. The man that picked me up asked where I was headed and why was I hitching a ride out here in the middle of New Mexico. I told him, adding that the bus had left just a few minutes before and was due to stop again in Amarillo. He said that he would just get close to the bus and follow it wherever it got off the highway. A few hours later I was back on the bus. God is good! In later years watching the TV program "Route 66," memories of this experience would pop into my head. The first bus ride was complete in Oklahoma City where I boarded another bus whose destination was Wichita, Kansas, with several stops on the way, including the City Drug Store in Pawnee. How nice! I could walk to the house from the bus stop. And I did, only to learn that Mom and Mary Sue were not living in it anymore. No one was at the house, so I walked to an aunt and uncle's house only a couple of blocks farther. My aunt called Mom about my arrival and then took me to the apartment where she and Mary Sue and Bonnie were living. After a happy reunion, I received instructions on when and where to appear in court and what the questions could be like, but not the exact questions. My arrival in Pawnee was either the 25th or 26th of October. The trial date was October 27th. So, lady luck was with us as far as timing was concerned. It seems we accomplished a lot because our date of marriage was October 29, 1958.

THE TRIAL SUMMARY

Pawnee County Court House Archives

Date of actual arrest unknown, but likely around October 20, 1958

Sources: County Court Records and the October 23 & 30, 1958

Issues of <u>The Pawnee Chief</u> weekly newspaper.

Hearing Date: October 23, 1958

Trial Date: October 27, 1958

Conviction Date: October 28, 1958

Sentencing Date: October 31, 1958

Delivered to Oklahoma State Penitentiary, McAlester, OK:
November 5, 1958

Subpoenas honored: Prosecution: 13   Defense: 7

Jury Deliberation about 3 hours, result, Conviction,

Statutory Rape in 2nd Degree

Sentence: 8 Years, Oklahoma State Prison, McAlester, OK.

(15 years is maximum)

Appeals filed: March 1959, Denied

WITNESSES AND TESTIMONY

If one assumes the Pawnee County Courthouse records to be accurate, prosecution witnesses outnumbered defense witnesses almost two to one. Whether that is important I don't know. What is important to me and my family is that X got "put away" for a while. He did not, however, receive the maximum sentence. Only one appeal is on the "record" and it was denied. As is recorded above, twenty subpoenas were honored. It follows then, that twenty people testified at this trial. My testimony was one of them – for the prosecution. My time "on the stand" most certainly was very brief compared to what I suppose was the case for my mother and my sister

Mary. Brother Mike's testimony, had he been available to give it, would also have been very lengthy and the final sentencing would likely have been considerably more severe – maybe even the full fifteen years for such a conviction. However, Mike's testimony about intent to kill (because the primary part of his testimony would have been concerned with the fact that X chased him with a rifle) could have resulted in an "attempted murder" charge being added to the rape charge. The prosecuting attorney, after confirming my name, relationship, et cetera, asked about the happenings on the day in the past summer when I entered the house unannounced and unexpected and was confronted by X.

I am unclear about how the lawyer knew about the incident and what was asked and answered and who was involved; but, at this writing, I assume the information came from Mary's testimony and/or other statements. I cannot recall the language specifically, but the following data is the essence of what happened in that confrontation with X. Having come to the house directly from my job at the drug store, I entered the house living room by the front door. I had tried the back door, but it was locked. Likely, door and screen-door noises announced my arrival since I was confronted by X within about thirty seconds. When he entered the living room from the "master" bedroom, he yelled at me: "What the hell are you doing here in the middle of the afternoon?"

The living room was separated from the master bedroom only by a common door in the west end of the north wall of the living room. The front door was on the south side of the house. The time of the day was early to mid-afternoon. I had moved toward the dining room table just inside the dining room archway when X appeared, and I was looking at an envelope I saw on the table. He wore only a pair of his work trousers. His hair was not its usual "slicked back" and he appeared to be sweating. The time of year, being early Fall, was about two months prior to my joining the U.S. Navy in late November. My response to his question was, "I got off work a little early, so I just came home." At that point I was working almost full time at the City Drug Store, and I had not yet been fully exposed to the military possibility. Also, Bonnie had agreed to live with and help a sister-in-law of hers who was pregnant with her third or fourth child in Kansas. Therefore, she was not close by for me to go see.

The prosecution attorney asked two or three clarifying questions and then turned me over to the defense lawyer whose queries I cannot recall with any specificity. Court records I reviewed for this writing did not include specific information about who testified, nor did it include names of people called to testify but did not, if any. Those records did reveal that thirteen witnesses were for the prosecution and seven for defense.

Part IV
Work and Family

CHAPTER 17

Marriage of Convenience?

Could you call ours a "marriage of convenience"? Certainly not, at least not in the original sense of such language. But it sure was convenient for us from a practical standpoint. For one thing, neither of our immediate families contained people with significant financial wealth at that time. Our families were, what I call "American Standard" (of the 1950s), i.e., working class with no notable accumulations of monetary wealth.

Here is another oddity, some people would say: The groom in this wedding (that would be me) had no earthly idea on arrival in town about when and where said wedding was to take place. In fact, I believe I didn't even know for certain "if" said wedding was to take place. It did, however, come to pass that the 29th of October was indeed "our" day in 1958, two days after my rendered testimony in X's trial. The way we managed to celebrate this event went something like this: The wedding ceremony was in the early afternoon. Afterward was gift unwrapping, ice cream and cake, and then a "spin" around town involving several other cars to sort of form a parade. I'm unaware of the genesis of the idea to "cruise" (at illegal speed) through town, even though I seemed to be the "leader" of the gang.

Problem was, the Pawnee Police did stop us for speeding. I got a ticket but nobody else did! Well, we were leaving town the next day anyway to go to Tulsa and catch a bus for San Diego. I have no idea what happened to that speeding ticket. It must have gotten packed in the little trunk which contained virtually all our earthly goods. Perhaps it, unknowingly, became part of a laundry load and thus disintegrated. I never saw the ticket again and nobody ever came to arrest me (or Bonnie). So, maybe it was just a ruse. I think it was when the Navy sent me to Vietnam seven years later that I quit worrying about that ticket and began to wonder if I would get back home.

SO, WHAT?

Emotions. Questions. Doubts. Misgivings. Amazement. Those were some of the experiences and conditions, expressed and unexpressed, that undoubtedly impacted my thoughts and actions, and Bonnie's too, as those four or five days around the trial progressed. While neither of us expressed negative thoughts or concerns about our wedding being squeezed in between all the other things, some of a highly negative nature, we somehow seemed to manage to come away with relatively good results. We believe God was certainly with us and helped us overcome any negative feelings or actions that could have happened under those circumstances. It seems quite likely that having to make some semblance of order out of what seemed to be chaos, and my obligation to get back to San Diego in a timely manner needed serious attention. At the same time, the need to try to make something meaningful out of our marriage event lingered in my mind, making me rather anxious about how all this was to happen.

Well, with all these dates and times flying around, I guess somebody just grabbed the 29th out of the air and reasoned that 2 P.M. seemed a reasonable time. Aunt Alma had already made decisions about punch and wedding cake and where to hold the reception – God bless her heart!

Whether that was the actual date and time of our wedding, I could not really validate. But it's the one we use. And it's the date on our marriage certificate. All I really knew about all the dates was that I needed to be back in San Diego and at the U.S. Naval Hospital on or before November 7th. We accomplished that – praise the Lord! Part of the irony of all of these activities is that X's imprisonment date was October 31 – that's Halloween, isn't it?

Bonnie and I, probably like most married couples, have certainly had our ups and downs. But we have somehow managed to overcome the "downs", or in some cases, learned to live with them and celebrate many of them. I must emphasize here that our ability to overcome conflict over any of our differences lies mostly with Bonnie. Her ability and willingness to forgive is considerably beyond mine. That does not, however, limit or impede her willingness and ability to stand up for herself.

Through the years our marriage has strengthened. It strengthened to the point that, despite the loss of our older son Michael in 1991 to suicide, we never so much as even discussed any sort of separation. We leaned heavily on one another and made corporate decisions about everything related to Michael's death. Divorce of parents who lose a child, particularly to suicide, is very common. We learned through counseling individually and in group sessions the need to learn to support each other. And that includes seeking even more of God in your life and admitting to yourself that you need help. Following is a glimpse of Michael's story.

MICHAEL

Michael made his appearance in our lives on September 4, 1959. That morning Bonnie was awakened very early, something like 3 a.m. or so with contraction pains. I went directly to Flo's unit (she had a telephone) to call a taxi. Within about half an hour we arrived at San Diego Naval Hospital delivery rooms. My workstation was in the same building, so I knew the area well. I got her into the delivery room area, and she was checked over quickly and put into a bed in a waiting area.

I was told it might take a while, so I should go find something to do or go home. In those years, husbands had little or no "rights" in delivery room areas; especially in military hospitals I suppose. So, as you can surmise, neither my job nor my familiarity with the doctors and nursing staff gained any preferential treatment. My work area, being very close-by, prompted me to start my workday early that day. Besides, what purpose would be served by my going to our apartment? After officially reporting for duty and changing to my "scrubs" (my work attire), I started doing whatever needed doing. However, after a while my curiosity got to me, so I put on a gown, cap and mask and headed for the room where Bonnie had been and learned she had just been taken to a delivery room. I headed for that room when I found out which one it was, entered it, and saw Bonnie on the table. My cap and mask and gown didn't fool anybody. They chased me out right away and told me to "never return," or something like that. At least I tried. Today it is an entirely different story. It seems I have heard that nowadays the whole family and close friends can gather to witness "the event." Whether they must "gown and cap" up, I do not know, but possibly not.

The next several days were delightful! Michael was given "celebrity" status in the nursery area. Balloons, crepe paper do-dads and ribbons adorned his crib. All the nursery nurses and hospital corps Waves competed for turns to hold and carry and even do diaper changes for Michael! The event of Michael's circumcision was a bit difficult to watch – but I was allowed to and did! I think he didn't care for it judging from his very loud complaint! It even made me feel a little anxious! Michael was a handful from the start. His was boundless curiosity, energy and appetite.

Apparent almost immediately after he began talking was that he had uncommon and tireless ability to learn. In grade school Michael was always at or near the top of his classes, earning him a spot in the school's gifted children's program. This opened doors that translated into even more open doors later. In college he did well, even on the football team. Mike, like most of our male family members, was below average in weight and height, but he still did well at football because he was a smart player at running back and linebacker positions. He was also courageous to a fault; much to his chagrin sometimes. After college, he taught school and coached for a few years and then joined the corporate world with the same company I had just retired from. I would not say that he had a "leg up" because of my tenure with the company. Instead, obvious to me and verifiable, was that he worked hard to get that position. Michael concentrated with precision to keep and excel in his work until his death by suicide in 1991.

THE LOSS

Today, twenty-seven years later, Bonnie and I still think of Michael daily. We do not dwell on the loss, but it is still quite painful at times, especially on anniversaries and common gathering times like Christmas and Thanksgiving. On a more positive note, Bonnie and I, after some special training, have been able to help other people who have suffered similar losses. That effort and work was a profound blessing to us as well. And we believe our faith in God and a lot of very hard grass-roots work on the recovery effort has helped us tremendously toward being able to live more-or-less "normal" lives – again, whatever "normal" means.

ROBERT

Robert came into our lives about fourteen months after Michael's arrival. Robert's birth occurred on November 2, 1960, in Tulsa, Oklahoma.

Early on it was clear that Robert shared Michael's level of curiosity and intelligence. One large difference between the two was Robert's level of patience. He developed a notable ability to think through and plan carefully and in detail and to take his time. He seems to have whatever it takes to exercise patience and be thorough in decision making. And his follow-through, I believe to be remarkable. Robert takes good care of himself, stays busy and has a very nice family life in which, thankfully, he is deeply involved. He and I worked together in our family business for over twenty years.

He, for the past several years, has worked elsewhere in a variety of businesses. Recently, however, he returned to his "business roots" and has opened a new business for himself. We pray for his success and we keep in contact – not for business necessarily (although we're interested), but just because it seems the proper thing to do. His family life includes having a great time keeping up with his grandchildren.

I am deeply gratified that he takes time to be interested in what Bonnie and I do and say and believe. He is always open to helping us when we need it. He is very interested in this writing project; mainly, I think, because he seems to see some potential in it. I hope he is right. I have a good feeling that he is indeed right! Currently, our plan is to do a visit together to the sawmill site, probably sometime in the fall months of 2020. We are very much looking forward to that trip and experience.

Of course, we have enjoyed a rather large number of trips that included Robert, many of those trips primarily having to do with "vacation" kinds of ventures. But Robert's first trip with us was in 1960, about six or seven weeks after his birth in Tulsa, Oklahoma. Because of seriously flawed planning due to inexperience in critical family matters, I had sent Bonnie "home" to Tulsa because my belief was that Bonnie and kids needed to be around family while I was to be aboard a Navy ship headed for Japan on January 3, 1961, and Robert was due soon! I don't quite recall all the thoughts and ideas; but for some now mysterious reason, we then decided Bonnie and kids really needed to be in San Diego because I was to be gone only about six months. Which turned out to be true.

I bought a used car in early December, took leave from the Navy, drove to Tulsa, picked up Bonnie and the kids, and headed back to San Diego, pulling a small trailer. We had "graduated" from just having a small trunk for our "stuff." Michael was 16 months old and Robert about six weeks old. Near Odessa, Texas, we got run off the road and hit a center median post on the divided highway. Three days later we were back on the road but had a transmission problem near Yuma, Arizona. Now, I was only a week away from the departure date of my ship bound for Japan. Missing ship's movement is a very serious offense, punishable by something just short of death, I think. Well, maybe not death, but certainly something not good.

A generous (to a fault) mechanic in Yuma got us back on the road, but only a few miles out, we broke down again. The mechanic (after I found a phone to call him) came to the rescue again, towed the car back to his shop, hooked my trailer onto his very nice pickup truck and told me to call him when we got to San Diego, and he would come get his pickup and return my car to me. He did not charge me for any of the repairs. I do not know his name, never thought to ask about his name, and I could not find his shop either because I have no recollection of where it is/was to begin with.

But, if you, Sir, happen to be reading this; and if you remember the red-headed U.S. Navy sailor with a wife and two very young kids and a broken-down car with a trailer stopping at your shop in late mid-December of 1960, please get in touch with me. I will probably remember your name when I hear it, and you would probably remember the car because of its make, model and color.

I did not have opportunity even to help Bonnie and the boys get settled into our little rent house. I think I probably shaved and showered and packed my sea bag, and headed for the ship almost immediately after unloading the pickup and returning the rental trailer. Robert says he remembers nothing of that trip! Imagine that. He was already over a month old. He should remember something! Shouldn't he?

ATTENTION CAR BUFFS!! Read this! I really, really, wish I still had that car I bought to go get Bonnie and the boys. Why? The year was 1960. I bought a 1957 Hudson Hornet Holiday. Colors: Red, White, Black with both silver and gold-color metal trim!! A two-door hardtop, V8, all power, no A/C. Of course, it was just a run-of-the-mill car "back then." I paid $700 for it! It purred like a kitten and drove as smooth as silk! I doubt I ever had a picture of it. So, I looked one up and printed it but, unfortunately, I could not find a red/white/black photo. But that's the car! I've read someplace that only about 600 of them were built. I sure wish I'd kept it!!

57' Hudson

———————— ✳ ————————

CHAPTER 18

Pharmacy School, Pharmacies and Pharmaceuticals

Scripture: My research for a scripture that addresses health or health care, or physical healing was at once revealing and confusing. Mindset here included but was not limited to physical healing. Biblical verses addressing healing seem to center more on spiritual healing, and when physical healing is addressed, the emphasis is on spirituality rather than on medicine per se'.

It was in my work, first as a Navy Hospital Corpsman/Pharmacy Technician followed by my tenure as a pharmaceutical products representative, that I encountered many physicians who, in addition to prescribing a treatment or medication, would also include his or her own prayer for healing of the patient. And, on two occasions, physicians (surgeons) who have cared for me have said their own prayers prior to the surgeries. They prayed not only for success of their surgical skills, but for the skilled use of process, medications, and the efforts of all attending physicians and technicians.

PHARMACY SCHOOL

Achieving enrollment into the USN Pharmacy School was a milestone for me. I started the application process in March 1958 and was approved and selected for enrollment by late November. My class started in very early January 1959 with 35 class members. Three of our instructors were trained pharmacy technicians who had attained E7 or higher rank and who were career Navy men. Another was of lower rank but held two degrees in medical sciences. He taught organic and inorganic chemistry. In charge was a Navy Lieutenant Commander in the Medical Service Corps with, I believe, a Medical Services type of degree. Our instructor for "pharmaceutical compounding" was one of the three Hospital Corps Chief Petty Officers. He "ran a tight ship," a favorite USN expression concerning efficiency and competency. The school term was almost a full year starting on 2 January 1959 and ending December 15.

We attended classes full-time, no breaks, no leaves granted, and observing legal holidays only. Long reading and study projects were assigned over nearly every weekend. We received courses in advanced Pharmacology and other pharmacy sciences of the time. We were fully introduced to the techniques, sciences, and mathematics of compounding pharmacy, learning to compound syrups, tinctures, ointments, oral capsuled preparations, and powders, among others.

From both physical and intellectual standpoints, the Compounding Pharmacy courses were, by far, the most difficult for some of our class members. One major reason for the high degree of difficulty was that, in those years, handheld calculators were not available. I think perhaps they had not even been thought of yet as a consumer product. So, all math calculations were done by pencil and paper. Exacerbating that problem was the fact that our math issues involved converting the various weight and volume systems, i.e., converting fluid ounces to cubic centimeters (or vice-versa) or grams or milligrams to ounces or fractions of ounces, or converting weights and measures from/to metric and avoirdupois and/or apothecary systems.

Two of our students could not overcome the difficulties of mastering weights and measures which, obviously, is critical to "compounding" pharmacy. Three other failures were probably due to less than good study habits. The top four students qualified for appointments to the U. S. Naval Academy or other avenues to achieve the commissioned ranks. Part of those qualification factors, as I understood it, included a grade-point average of 3.75 or higher on a 4.0 scale. I missed the "cut," but was close enough to receive "honorable mention" and fifth place with a 3.68 GPA.

Bonnie and I made no trips to the wonderful beach areas of San Diego during the entire school session. We may have gone to one movie. I did, however, find time occasionally to play a chess game or two with Flo and others. It is safe to say that this course was close to the equivalent of a two-year college schedule. And as most of us had already learned, when you join the Navy, it's a 24/7 commitment. All selectees had to meet several required qualification standards including any past school records, I.Q. kinds of criteria (they called it GCT/ARI) which stands for General Comprehension Test and Math, and, of course, "clean" records regarding performance, discipline, and related issues.

A WESTPAC CRUISE

The month of December 1959 signaled the end of and graduation from pharmacy school and preparations to go aboard the destroyer tender, USS Prairie AD-15, to assume control of the ship's Pharmacy. Using my infinite wisdom, near the end of pharmacy school, I had made the decision to send Bonnie (about 7 months pregnant with Robert and having Michael in tow) to Tulsa, Oklahoma, to reside with my mother and to birth Robert.

(This story is in "Robert's" section of the previous chapter.) It is the story of our mad rush to get everybody back to San Diego. I have yet to understand the logic of sending Bonnie and Michael to Tulsa in order to be with "family" (while I was to be overseas) and to give birth to Robert somewhere other than San Diego. No animosity here, just the idiotic stupidity and lack of understanding and courage and common sense that resulted in Bonnie's travel to Tulsa and then my retrieving her. So, dear reader, just don't ask! OK? So, I feel a little better now. I've vented my frustration and admitted my infantile stupidity and fantastic lack of "common sense," decision making

WESTPAC stands for West Pacific in USN terminology, and it identifies a general global area of fleet activity. My ship's primary mission was to maintain a certain group or groups of fleet destroyers and destroyer escorts; our ship was a destroyer tender, a type of ship tasked with maintenance and repair functions for destroyer-type war ships. Her name was U.S.S. Prairie (AD-15). At this writing Prairie has long since been retired and scrapped, perhaps making memories of that cruise more significant than they might otherwise be.

Time Out! I've used the word "cruise" a few times in this story. I need you to understand that "cruise" in this military setting has nothing to do with luxurious sleeping quarters, highbrow living and dining spaces, nor being served cocktails in the early afternoon, and relaxing under the palm trees on a beach of white sand. "Cruise" simply means to move the ship from one setting to another and has very little to do with sightseeing and related activity. Just so you know! However, I seem to recall people on board USN ships commenting on the ship's captain's quarters being rather luxury oriented and with a well-stocked liquor cabinet.

A special memory for me on this cruise was when the USS Black (DD 666) came along side to receive fuel and supplies from Prairie while we were underway. Quite a maneuver to witness. Because of her hull number (666), she was labeled "Devil Ship" by many sailors, and some sailors, I heard years later, would refuse to serve on her because of the nickname and/or hull number! Several ships of other classes do or did have hull number 666, but I could learn of no other destroyer or related classes of ships that do or did.

I wish I had had access to salvage when Prairie was decommissioned. My ship's pharmacy featured stainless-steel cabinetry, shelves, and countertops. The countertop cabinet contained forty-five small drawers and six larger ones and two pull-out work surfaces. All stainless steel. Just keep it clean and it shines! Up to this point in my Navy service, except for "Boot Camp," I had not been exposed to much of the "military" aspect of being a member of the US Navy. Shipboard duty exposes every sailor to the basics of tradition and ceremony and seamanship of military service in the United States Navy. And I am proud of having had that opportunity. Then, a few years later, my service as a hospital corpsman stationed with U.S. Marine Corps units intensified my pride in our military services. Duty with the Marines meant we wore the Marine Corps uniform, something we all took a great deal of pride in. And on this subject, I feel obligated to make clear that once a "navy guy" (or gal) has been assigned to duty with Marine Corps units, he/she will generally choose to stay with Marine Corps duty if given the choice. The obvious question by some regarding the previous statement is: Why? The answer is "respect."

When a hospital corpsman stationed with a Marine Corps unit needs something not already available, you just find one of your Marine friends and ask. This is particularly true for those of us serving with the "grunts" – the ground troops deployed into war zones where the grunts go to extra efforts to help protect their "doc" – the main effort being concentrated on making their "doc" look and act just like the rest of them. The corpsman is not asked to wear gear emblazoned with a red cross inside a white circular surface nor to carry gear that would identify him/her as a medic. My understanding is that our war with North Korea proved that point and Vietnam verified the point. When any of us "docs" in my unit were assigned to be on patrol or on a field mission, usually an AR15 or a "grease gun" was made available, and we just left our .45 pistol behind. But, to be clear, I was rarely asked/ordered to go out on missions, primarily because of my first duty being my pharmacy chores. And just as a note of interest (to me at least), one of the first things I was assigned to do when our unit arrived in Vietnam was to design and build my own pharmacy! I had a lot of help and our base camp area was considered quite secure – compared to other assignments I might have been given. And it saddened me considerably when I learned that not very long after my departure from Vietnam that our "medical" facility was almost completely destroyed in a raid. I do not know if any of my fellow corpsmen friends lost lives, but possibly so.

SOME CHINA FOR BONNIE

So, back to the 1960 WESTPAC cruise we were about to embark on. We visited ports in the Philippine Islands, Borneo, Hong Kong, and others in the South China Sea. Our home port, however, was Yokosuka, Japan, where I purchased an eight-place setting of china and accompanying tableware for Bonnie. I found all of it in Yokosuka by following recommendations from shipmates, one of them our doctor, for the china shops I should visit. A few hours of looking resulted in settling on the Noritake brand and the Besse pattern. The purchase made, and an eight-place setting of tableware also under an arm, I made my way back to the dock area to await a ride out to the ship which was at anchor about two miles distant. Finally, a "Prairie" boat made dock and a group of ten or twelve other sailors and I clambered on board, and in a hurry because rain had started falling. I clearly remember becoming very concerned about the weather issue when the rain became more intense, and we were still a mile away from the ship. Several problems were on the horizon for me: 1. Regulation "Navy Blues" were then (and presumably still are) 100 or almost 100 percent wool. 2. I had no rain gear with me. 3. I had about 60 or 70 lbs. of china and tableware. 4. My own 140 lbs. of body weight. 5. I had something close to thirty feet of ladder (narrow stairway with a right-hand siderail) up the side of the ship at a steep angle to climb to access the main deck after clumsily exiting the boat. 6. Everybody else on the boat was (or seemed to be) carrying packages. 7. I'm a nice guy. I let all the others leave in front of me even though I probably outranked some of them. 8. I got a break here! One of the boat crew offered to help me with my packages while I got on the ladder platform. 9. Here's the scenario for this part of this event: The ship is at anchor but relatively stable because of size and weight while the boat we were exiting is moving up and down with the sea waves – so you must time your exit from the boat to coincide with the availability of the ship's ladder platform. The rise and fall of the boat riding the waves was at least four feet. The water was getting rougher because of the storm! 10. Next was the job of climbing the ladder with<u>out</u> the use of my hands to grip the chain/rail – so it was a balancing act. It took a while. Whew! I think my heart rate increased just writing this scene. It is, then, that this eight-place setting of Noritake "Besse" moved from Japan to San Diego, CA, to Santa Ana, CA, to Garden Grove, CA (three addresses), to Wilmington, DE, and finally to Edmond, OK, before it ever got its own cabinet! This means it stayed boxed up from early in 1961 until late in 1979 when we finally purchased a beautiful china cabinet! Bonnie says we unpacked the china and tableware one time for use sometime during that eighteen-year period. The event must surely have been something special!

PHARMACIES

My first assignment out of pharmacy school was aboard the destroyer tender U.S.S. Prairie (AD15). Then I went to the heavy cruiser U.S.S. St. Paul (CA73). These were "independent duty" types of assignments, i.e., no registered pharmacist on board these ships. I had sole responsibility for all things related to the operation of the shipboard pharmacy, but under the command of the senior Medical Officer on board. The rest of my 10 plus years of service was in other assignments including the base hospital pharmacy at El Toro Marine Corps Air Station. I deployed to Vietnam for 14 months in June of 1966 where I was part of a "start-up" group with a Marine Corps air wing. Part of my job in Vietnam was to help physically build our "medical facility." I'm glad I already knew the nuts and bolts of hard physical work. The sun was sure hot! And the torrential rains were sure cold! To tell you a bunch of "sea stories" here would be easy – but I am putting them into a different writing project. However, I will spin a couple of my favorites out for your enjoyment. They are both brief.

The first concerns narcotic inventories aboard ship. My first "sea duty" assignment was the USS Prairie, the destroyer tender based out of San Diego. This was also my first "independent duty" Pharmacy assignment. A USN Destroyer Tender is a ship designed to accomplish certain maintenance and repairs and other services and supplies for destroyer type ships, as mentioned earlier. Often, when in port and/or at anchor, a tender will have several such ships tied up alongside for those services. On January 2, 1961, (a very short time after finally arriving back in San Diego from Tulsa, Oklahoma, with Bonnie and the boys and getting them settled), I reported aboard USS Prairie for this first independent duty assignment. The ship left port the following morning bound for Japan. I had, the day before, signed off on the ship's Pharmacy inventory which included several controlled substance drugs, meaning narcotics and alcohol, but not including barbiturates or other similar drugs such as dextroamphetamine containing products (for weight control in those years and highly abused these days). My pharmacy was equipped with all the necessary tools and appliances to complete almost any compounding need that might arise. These tools included a very nice (and new) torsion balance or, as some prefer, gram scale. One morning a few days after departing Hawaii bound for Yokosuka, Japan, the Executive Officer of the ship appeared with two other ship's officers, at my pharmacy window saying they needed to complete a narcotics and controlled drug inventory. This would, by necessity, require the use of the torsion balance since several of those products were in "bulk" packaging, some of which had been opened. A torsion balance, to be accurate, needs a solid stable base. Key word here is "stable." A ship at sea is not stable – at least not to the degree needed to get an accurate reading on a gram scale (one type being a torsion balance). It took a while for me to convince the Commander that they needed to wait till we made harbor in Yokosuka and await a calm day, to complete this chore. I remember sometimes wondering about college graduates, especially when they become military officers – unless, of course, they are Naval Academy or West Point graduates! Nonetheless, I always respected higher military rank, regardless of my personal feelings. Most, I believe, got where they were through hard work.

By the way, if you are wondering, for me to accomplish any compounding that required the use of the torsion balance, I too, had to wait for a calm day in port. Can't do it when at sea! These were solid and liquid measurements measured in milligrams and cubic centimeters, not pounds and pints or even ounces of weight or volume. A fluid ounce contains 29.5 (roughly!) cubic centimeters – that's volume. An ounce of solid substance weighs 28.35 grams. A milligram is 1/1000 of a gram. Here is another exercise to illustrate size/weight perspective. One of my Rx products is in a 25 mg. (milligram) tablet. It takes forty (40) of those tablets to weigh one gram of active ingredient. The prescribed dose is one tablet per day, so one ounce of active ingredient is approximately a four-week supply of therapy! Perhaps those numbers put things in better perspective.

Following my "sea duty" days aboard two different ships for a couple of years, I received orders to report to El Toro Marine Corps Air Station Base Hospital near Santa Ana, California – some 20 or 30 miles southeast of Los Angeles. Of special significance to me and my family, still today, is that this assignment put Bonnie and me in a place that allowed us to "spread out" a bit. We established our first "Sandisize" in Garden Grove, California. This is discussed in more detail in the following chapter. We also bought our first two homes in Garden Grove, CA. My rank then was HM2, having attained that aboard ship. While at El Toro, I worked in three different departments, each having some relationship to pharmaceuticals. One of the sections was a place for military dependents to obtain (at cost) drugs not available in the base hospital pharmacy. This was great duty. I was home most nights (except for a one-month tour of "night duty"). Otherwise, I was busy filling prescriptions. One significant memory I have of that time was the day I was filling a prescription for Ortho Novum, a birth control product, for a young woman named Annie A. About noon an announcement over the PA system blared out: "Attention all hands. Attention all hands. You are hereby informed that the President of the United States, President John F. Kennedy, has been shot in Dallas, Texas. At this time, we are unaware of his condition, but it is believed he was shot in the head. The President is in an emergency room in Dallas, Texas. We will inform you of conditions as they are reported to us." Date - November 22, 1963, a day many have never forgotten. Then on June 25, 1965, an airplane with a full load of Marines headed for Vietnam crashed into the low mountains just east of the El Toro runways. My involvement in this event was as part of a body identification team. It was a gruesome and unforgettable assignment. About a year later I received orders to report to a Marine Corps group on its way to Vietnam.

Another matter I believe worthy of comment took place later in 1965 when a Navy Commander in charge of personnel matters pertaining to all of us Navy guys and gals needed a favor from me. The Commander had sent one of his enlisted guys (a Yeoman 1st Class – one rank higher than mine) to take possession of the typewriter I used for prescription labels.

He (the Commander) wanted it to use in his task of designing another one of his forms. The reason he needed my typewriter was because of its extremely small typeface. It was an ultra-micro-elite, something like sixteen or eighteen characters per inch – thus very nice for typing prescription labels – considering the wordiness of some of the doctors. I told the yeoman I had fifteen or twenty prescription labels to finish and would probably have forty or fifty the following day – so I could not be without my typewriter for more than a few hours -and that the commander could have it sometime the next day for a couple of hours. In fact, I was typing labels as we talked, so the Yeoman knew I was busy with it – he persisted but I held my ground.

The following morning as I was entering the building, I heard over the PA system: "HM2 Romack, report immediately to the Commander's office. On the double! He is waiting for you!" Somebody was watching for me! After getting my rear end chewed on for a while by the Commander, I explained, when he gave me a moment for rebuttal, that I fill fifty or more special order prescriptions every day for military dependents, and each one must have legible instructions on very small labels, so I could not be without a typewriter that would let me do that. The Commander seemed to back off a bit saying he understood my position but that I needed to consider his need also. I remember thinking something like – is the Commander wanting to bargain with me? So, I offered the information that my slowest times for typewriter use were usually early in the day and often about a two-hour period in the mid-afternoons. Well, we worked it out.

About three years later on April 1, 1968 as I mustered out of the Navy following my tours of duty in Vietnam and San Diego, I was given all my personnel and health records files. Just a few weeks ago, as I reviewed some of those records preparing for this segment of my writing, I found the last two performance reports from El Toro base hospital duty. Both reports were signed by the Commander and both reports were straight 4.0 scores. That's as good as it gets! His written comments were very complimentary. How nice! As an added piece of information about the Commander, I offer this: The initials for his first and middle names are/were S and F. His most common signature was: S. F. Last Name followed by rank and title. The Armed Services are all big on monikers, acronyms, titles, and forms – and abbreviations. And one of these military forms is simply Standard Form (####). And that's how it would be listed in a catalogue. Well, put two and two together...Oh! You already have! Well, good! But what I'm really wondering about is whether the Commander ever put it together. I am quite aware that most of us corpsmen "put it together" because we always abbreviated "Standard Form" with "SF" and then the number.

As an independent duty Pharmacy Technician those last several months in San Diego, part of my job was to see pharmaceutical sales reps who worked for companies that had contracts with the military. This became an opportunity for exposure to a good number of pharmaceutical firms via meeting their sales representatives. Therefore, I had ample opportunity to "interview them" which helped me decide to which firms I would apply. I had achieved multiple interviews with multiple companies before my termination date from the Navy. Still residing in one of my file cabinets is a folder containing data about all thirty-five (35) pharmaceutical manufacturers to which I applied and the replies from them. I completed almost all of my initial interviews before mustering out of the Navy. This enabled me to complete all second and third interviews and be employed within just a few days over thirty days from my discharge date. So it was that I became a sales representative for Stuart Pharmaceuticals in early March 1968. It was one of four offers and is known today as AstraZeneca. Separation from the military in 1968 seemed a never-ending process. Maybe it was because my separation date was April Fool's Day that things seemed to be so drawn out. Possibly, if we had not still been deeply involved in Vietnam, I might have "stayed for 20" as they say. God, as it turned out, had better plans. One thing that confirms God's involvement in my "retirement" issue is that the pharmaceutical firm I worked for has a good retirement program. My tenure with that company was only eleven years, but the retirement benefit from that work is almost the same as what my military benefit would have been had I stayed for 20 years. And I still qualify for and receive veteran's benefits too. God is good!

PHARMACEUTICALS

In the 1960s and 70s, Pharmaceutical Companies were considerably more numerous than today in 2019. Part of that scenario was that competition was very high because the high number of companies meant a high number of competing products – often the same products but with different trade names. Consequently, field sales staffs, for direct contact with prescribing physicians, pharmacists and wholesalers, meant a lot of jobs. For instance, simple over the counter products like antacids, laxatives, prenatal vitamins and cough preparations, were all promoted heavily through physicians (in those days we had no high-level television advertising for "over the counter" drugs). The same was true for prescription drugs as well, because of patent expiration which allowed other drug companies to manufacture and market the same drug under different trade names. Thus, competition included the use of "detail men" (women began joining the ranks in the middle 1970s). This circumstance often would become fodder for a good, even friendly, relationship with competing sales representatives. For instance, I became good friends with the "Maalox guy" and with the "Isordil guy," my most serious competitors. But these were relationships that sometimes even involved spouses via family "get-togethers." Antagonism was indeed rare, thankfully! God blessed us with a couple of promotions that involved two relocations which took my family and me from Orange County, California, to Wilmington, Delaware, and then to Oklahoma City. The company (AstraZeneca) from whom I receive a retirement check each month, as it is formed now, has become a world leader in the discovery, production and marketing of significant pharmaceuticals. I'm quite sure I have no personal acquaintances still employed by the firm. However, it seems highly likely that a number of the folks I knew and worked with achieved significant positions within the corporation.

CHAPTER 19

Sandisize

The labor of the righteous leads to life, the wages of the wicked to sin.
Proverbs 10:16 (NKJV)

Sandisize, as a business name, was for a Janitorial/Custodial service I began in Garden Grove, California, while stationed as a Navy Pharmacy Tech with the base hospital at the (then) El Toro Marine Corps Air Station near Santa Ana, California, in 1963. By that time, Bonnie and I had two children, and we needed more money than my Navy pay. My deployment to Vietnam caused the demise of that business, the discontinuance of its name, and the income from it. The name Sandisize came from combining parts of three related words: Sanitize, Disinfect, and Deodorize. The second use of the name lasted for almost 30 years starting very early in 1980 in Edmond, Oklahoma, following early retirement from AstraZeneca. We established a flooring installation and floor care business which was finally closed in 2009. For that venture we revived the name "Sandisize" and added to it "of Edmond." This year, 2018, our son Robert has reestablished the business, so Sandisize of Edmond lives again!

HOW IT BEGAN

By late 1962 I had achieved the rank of HM2 and was soon to be assigned to the hospital pharmacy at El Toro Marine Corps Air Station (as noted early in Chapter 18). I also, eventually, became involved in what we called the Outpatient Purchasing section of the base hospital pharmacy at El Toro, discussed in the previous chapter. Although my rank was E5, my military pay was not keeping up with my idea of my family needs. Our two sons were ages three and four and the year was 1963. My solution to that issue was the formation of a small "office cleaning" business. I then made some decisions about services we would offer and some ideas about what kinds of businesses we would target. With those things in mind, I queried several of my "buddies" at the base to work with me on a part-time basis. Then I purchased supplies and equipment. It wasn't very complicated. I then took a few days of "leave time" and went looking for work. I found customers and selected one of my buddies to work with me (Bonnie did too from time to time, but her priority was the care of our sons.) We ran our little business for a little over two years before I received orders for duty in Vietnam. My first "Sandisize" vehicle was a 1963 Chevrolet "two-ten," four-door sedan. It was also our "family car." It had a very large trunk and a six-cylinder engine. I guess we probably did not quite create a strictly "professional" image with three or four guys in the car and a trunk full of brooms, mops, scrub machine (buffer) and buckets along with gallon jugs of concoctions and boxes or bags of granular items for cleaning windows and floors and commodes and sinks. But we were off to a great start!

ANOTHER "SANDISIZE" TIMES TWO

A little bit of recap here might be useful to help maintain continuity. Following duty in Vietnam and then the pharmacy at Naval Station, San Diego, was my discharge from the U.S. Navy. Then came my years with

Stuart Pharmaceuticals/AstraZeneca and first retirement. The "corporate world" is okay but my makeup is much more independent than the "average guy," I think. At any rate, I was itching to restart Sandisize. So, that's what Bonnie and I did. I could not have gotten it done without her help, her backing, and her involvement. This change resulted in the formation of another Sandisize, this one labeled "Sandisize of Edmond" (Oklahoma,) and our work was the sales and installation and care of multiple types of flooring. Over the years we made some money, wore out several pickups and vans, hired some people, fired some, and through the Grace of God, generally had a "good run." We enjoyed a very good reputation and accumulated a "book of memories," so to speak. But the resounding significance of this venture was when our son, Robert, relocated to Edmond, Oklahoma, from Wilmington, Delaware to join us in our business. I needed help and Robert needed work. That's what the Romack family, like many American families, is all about; work and productivity and engagement in community. I turned the business over to Robert in 2004 and he shut it down in 2009.

I just now got off the phone with Robert. He had called to find out if I had plans for the Ford van I bought a couple of years ago to help with my photography. I asked why he was asking. He said he wants to buy it so he can reopen Sandisize...again! Good Heavens! What a surprise! His intent is to continue the company name "Sandisize of Edmond" unless some of our quirky laws prohibit that move. Edmond, Oklahoma, has grown in population steadily for these past thirty plus years, so Robert has a good base to work with. His faith in God along with his workmanship and positive personality, will serve him well, I am sure.

CHAPTER 20

Reflection

FROM THE SAWMILL TO "THE SAWMILL"

As Bonnie and I proceed into our eighth decades of life and our sixth decade of marriage, we cannot avoid being eternally thankful to our Lord for the good lives we've enjoyed together. Nor can we avoid being thankful for God's presence in those months and years of significantly difficult conditions under which we both lived in our youth and teenage years. Bonnie's was a life of abject poverty until she was sent to live with an aunt and uncle who put her and her closest sister through high school. My life included, of course, circumstances and events recorded herein. We both believe we each attained many strengths and understandings that have been beneficial to us and which likely could not have been attained under "normal" lifestyles. Again, whatever "normal" means. Living and working at the sawmill in the northern mountains of New Mexico in 1950-51 was indeed an unforgettable experience that seriously and harshly impacted the lives of my siblings and me.

Oddly, or perhaps thankfully, neither Mary nor I have any recall of even preparing to leave the mountains, much less making the trip to Oklahoma from the Iron Spring Canyon sawmill in the southeastern corner of the far northwest section of Carson National Forest in New Mexico. The same was true for brother Mike. Donna June, being only a year and a half old at the time of the departure from the sawmill, has no recollection of the time. But she has, over the years, been made knowledgeable of many of the details, mostly by Mom and Mary. As discussed in Chapter 13, the time element between leaving the mountains and arriving in Pawnee, Oklahoma, was akin to a time warp to us three, likely due to drug implementation. And, as stated before in this writing, Laudanum, an opioid sedative, was commonly available in those years along with several other now restricted stimulant and sedative products. I suggest the use of Laudanum during this trip primarily because neither I nor any of my siblings have (or had) any recall of that move and no recall of the actual road trip to Pawnee. That trip could have been fast and furious, or it could have taken a week or more, given the strong possibility of car problems and the fact of non-existent high-speed multilane highways in 1951. My sense is that this car trip from Iron Spring in western North Central New Mexico to Pawnee in the western part of the northeast quadrant of Oklahoma, in probably late September or early October 1951, some 800 to 900 miles, could have been via Route 64 out of Dulce in northern New Mexico or Highway 66 from Albuquerque. Neither of those two routes was complete through all of Oklahoma, Texas and/or New Mexico in 1950. (Highway 64 enters Oklahoma from New Mexico at the west end of the Oklahoma panhandle. Therefore, you can completely avoid being in Texas, if that is your wish!) Either way meant a long trip with lots of stops. We likely made no hotel/motel stops, and slept, ate, and drank in the car. I suspect we made "opportune" potty stops only, making it possible to have completed the trip in as little as two or three days.

It seems appropriate to believe that Mom and her four offspring were, at least for a time, happy to be on the road away from the sawmill. Little did we know, however, that this was not the end of the story, but only a continuation of it, as you have read. Not recorded herein thus far is conversation about the last fifteen plus years. So, I'll fill you in now and hopefully illustrate its relevance to *The Sawmill*.

Here we go! Bonnie and I both decided to start receiving Social Security at age 65. So that was about fifteen years ago. My! How time flies! Let me "explain" a little about Bonnie. First, she only sits still when she is watching her favorite television show. Notice, "show" is singular. She only watches one besides the news. The rest of the time she is physically busy; washing clothes, cooking, cleaning (except she doesn't dust). When dusting is done, I do it but not very often. She likes to shop, and she sees regularly every Wednesday morning, a care-receiver she's been seeing for eleven years at this writing. Bonnie also enjoys doing little "craft" kinds of things and then gives her "products" away, usually in our church setting. I do not sit still either. I just can't do it! I've rebuilt our kitchen, built a very nice black-walnut pantry, built and replaced all book shelving in the den, and many other similar chores. I cannot just sit and watch TV or read, although I love to read, but I do that for an hour or so before bed. We travel when we can afford it, and our trips are not just to one place or site or event. We do month long trips and over the years we've been (by car) in every continental state. We have flown to Alaska and Hawaii. So, we are both quite busy in our retirement. My photography is better than mediocre, so I print and frame a lot of it. Oh yes, we are both still busy with a few church-related things.

As you have already read, my brother and I decided in 1971 to meet at the sawmill area (which he finally found just by roaming the mountains in his 4 wheel). That visit seems to have planted a seed that finally started growing a year or two ago and has grown into this book. Since you are reading right now what I've written, I guess we had success in getting it published! How about that?! Bonnie and I appreciate your having read this story. We hope it has been a blessing to you. And I hope you have not been bored, chagrined, disappointed, or unduly challenged by my sometimes clumsy or awkward attempts at humor. In my own defense of these attempts, at least I have not tried to complete any sort of intellectual or sophisticated humor! However, if some of it looks or sounds to be either intellectual or sophisticated, or both, it is purely accidental and unplanned!

Bonnie will tell you I like to tell stories. I do. My conversational skills are pretty good. Sadly, however, my hearing is fading away, so vocal conversation is harder now. I did well in the Pharmaceutical Sales business and running a small owner/operator business later, so I can communicate reasonably well. But I love telling stories. All I need is for someone to listen, or to read. Herein, hopefully, you will have found stories and stories inside of stories which, I believe, is part of any well written story. Which, presumably, is one reason why we break stories into chapters and subchapters. You, I hope, have found this narrative to be largely conversational and serious in tone. Injection of humor, however, is important to me, even in a serious setting. I have tried to spread it around in bits and pieces. And I hope I haven't bored you with it. Planning humor spots seems to be not possible for me, anyway. They seem to just happen. I believe God directs us toward, at least sometimes, being lighthearted. And I believe He will correct me if I put something where it should not be. I also believe that God will sometimes laugh with us. Therefore, even in an extremely serious setting, we can inject some appropriate thoughts of humor that might help to "lighten the load," as it were.

———————— ✳ ————————

AFTERWORD

If brother Mike were still alive and if we talked about some of our experiences, we would both have something quirky, cute, funny, contemplative, sad, downright outrageous, and even angry, to say about our experiences at the sawmill and the aftermath of it. That would most likely be cleansing, maybe even pleasing.

ABOUT THE AUTHOR

Work life for brother Mike and me, started early at the sawmill at age eleven for me and nine and one half for Mike. This story has told you much more about that. Making good grades later in school for us both in Pawnee, OK, happened despite our continuation of work outside of school. Neither of us participated to any serious extent in school sports or other extracurricular activities of any significance. Newspaper delivery and yard work for neighbors taught Mike and me more about early hours and hot sweaty work. We already knew about cold freezing work.

My job as a drugstore soda jerk taught me something more about dealing with people. Two seasons of raising turkeys taught us more about working when necessary; day or night, rain or shine, heat or cold, and snow. Our military experience taught us about our wonderful country and patriotism, and yes, about more discipline in our work. As a U.S. Navy Hospital Corpsman, and a pharmacy technician and, later, a pharmaceutical sales representative, I learned even more about discipline, dealing with people, and higher attention to detail in my work.

While working as a pharmaceutical business market researcher, I learned more about stringing words together. As owner and operator of a flooring sales and service company, I learned more about dealing with a customer base and better time management. As a school bus driver (What? a school bus driver? Yep! I did. And I earned a training certificate too! It is a great "retirement" job with summers off and six-hour days, if that's what you choose.) My lessons learned were about dealing with young people in a world of seemingly hyper confusion and oft times lack of discipline. As an aspiring author of nonbusiness writing, I've learned that I didn't know much at all about writing stories! So, since you are reading this, perhaps I can rest easy that I have achieved some degree of success as an author of nonbusiness writing! And please know that I happily undertook this project of writing *The Sawmill* trusting in God and myself and leaning on the support of my entire family, but especially my wife Bonnie, my two sisters Mary and Donna, and a small circle of friends and other relatives and acquaintances, and my PROOFREADERS! My hope for this book is that it might inspire someone to "tough it out" and lean on God when things are hard and, perhaps, along the way lead that someone to a God-inspired and blessed life, or enhance the life they already have with Him. Bonnie and I (by the time of your reading this story) have celebrated 60 years of marriage. We began dating in High School, therefore, Bonnie has some firsthand knowledge of nearly all the things presented herein. She gave birth to our son Michael in 1959 and Robert in 1960. We have two grandchildren and four step-grandchildren. Great-grandchildren number nine at last count. I worked in the pharmaceutical world for over twenty years, then in a private flooring business for about 30 years. I capped off my work life by driving for the school system for a few years – mentioned earlier - possibly one of my most challenging endeavors when you consider having to attempt to manage other people's children! We have, for all our married life, been active in and supportive of our church family.

The lowest point in my life was the loss by suicide of our older son Michael, in 1991. My deployment to Vietnam in 1966 with a Marine Corps unit and leaving my two sons and wife to fend for themselves for over 14 months was a very low point. I am, however, very proud to have served for almost 6 years with the U. S. Marine Corps as a U. S. Navy Hospital Corpsman. My total Navy time was 10 years, 6 months. On a much brighter note, I am extremely proud of our son Robert. He is a "man's man" and a good family man. He takes good care of his family. He is devoted to his wife Patty and is honorable in his dealings with other people. Expressing myself is much easier by the written word. In speaking, I tend to get forgetful, frustrated, apprehensive, disjointed, and off subject easily. In spite of all that, I was a successful pharmaceutical sales representative, and going on in that business into market research and even some experience in clinical research documentation in the animal health industry, and finally a district sales manager. Someday I may find a job I can stick with! Bonnie and I have made our home in Oklahoma, since 1970.

CLAUDE E. ROMACK CHRONOLOGY

Year	Grade	Age	Location	Activities
1946	1	7	Colo. Springs	School, cops & robbers, Superman
1947	2	8	Albuquerque	Snakes, Frogs, Mexican Kids
1948	3	9	Pawnee, OK	Aunt Alma, Uncle Charlie, Hound Dogs
1949	4	10	Albuquerque	Horses, Camping, Motor Cycle, Broken Leg
1950	5	11	Albuquerque	To sawmill in May or June

Missing Grade 5 and part of Grade 6

Year	Grade	Age	Location	Activities
1951	6	12	Sawmill, then the move to Pawnee, OK,	entering Grade 6 in October or early November 1951
1952	7	13	Pawnee, OK	Scrap Metal, pop bottles, grass cutting, odd jobs
1953	8	14	Pawnee, OK	Grass mowing, newspaper deliveries
1954	9	15	Pawnee, OK	Grass mowing, newspaper deliveries and hatchery work
1955	10	16	Pawnee, OK	Turkey farm, serious study sessions
1956	11	17	Pawnee, OK	Turkey farm, study, soda jerk work
1957	12	18	Pawnee, OK	Drug Store, HS Graduation, enter USN

ADULT YEARS

1958 — U S Navy Hospital Corps School, Hospital Ward Duty, Nursery Formula Room, The Trial, Marriage on October 29, 1958

1959 — San Diego Naval Hospital, Nursery Formula room and Autoclave Room, Michael's birth September 4, 1959

1960 — Robert's birth, Tulsa, OK on Nov. 2, Graduated Pharmacy School in December

1961 to 68 — Sea duty aboard USS Prairie (AD15), USS St. Paul (CA73), then El Toro USMC Air Station, Santa Ana, Base Hospital Pharmacy; Open Purchase Pharmacy; Medical Stores; MAG (Marine Air Group) 13, Chu Lai, South Vietnam; U.S. Naval Base, San Diego, Discharged from USN on April Fool's Day, 1968

1969 to 80 — Stuart Pharmaceuticals (now Astra Zeneca) sales rep, market researcher, Animal Health market research, District Sales Manager

1980 to 2006 — Owner/Operator of a floor-care and sales company

1991 — The loss by suicide of our son Michael

2006 to Present — Pseudo Retirement, Church stuff, Photography, Writing, Travel

2018 — Celebrated 60th Wedding Anniversary, October 29!

2019 — Published this book! *The Sawmill*

IMAGE INDEX